LANGUAGE AND TEXTS

The Nature of
Linguistic Evidence

Essays by

Robert P. Austerlitz

David R. Shackleton Bailey

James Barr

I. J. Gelb

Mary Haas

Reinhold Merkelbach

Morse Peckham

Chaim Rabin

Commentaries by

Judah Goldin

Albert H. Marckwardt

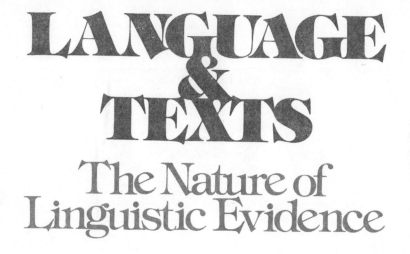

LANGUAGE & TEXTS
The Nature of Linguistic Evidence

Edited by Herbert H. Paper

Center for Coördination of Ancient and Modern Studies
The University of Michigan
Ann Arbor

Typed by Peg Hayman.

Library of Congress Catalog Card No. 75-36885

ISBN 0-915932-02-4

Cover design by Bill Howison, senior graphic artist, University of Michigan Publications.

CONTENTS

CONTENTS

FOREWORD

This book contains the papers written for our symposium on "Language and Texts" in March of 1974. Prof. Paper, the Editor, in his modest but engaging Introduction (below, p. ix), tells the story of how that conference came to be held; my part is simply to indicate how it, and the book to which it has given rise, are related to the purposes of the Center for Coördination of Ancient and Modern Studies.

The Center was established at the University of Michigan in 1969, as a sounding board, message center, and catalytic agent to promote and encourage every worthwhile mode of coöperation between ancient and modern studies—"ancient" as used here meaning primarily though not exclusively Graeco-Roman civilization and the ancient Near East, and "modern" referring mainly but not solely to the Western world since the Middle Ages.

The most important single device the Center has used in its pursuit of this aim was a series of four major (and several minor) multi-disciplinary conferences organized around themes which spanned the two time-frames; and the fruits of those conferences are now being garnered in a series of three books currently in process of publication. First to be published, in September 1975, was *JANUS: Essays in Ancient and Modern Studies,* edited by Louis L. Orlin and containing selected essays and discussion from two conferences mounted in 1973, *The City in History: Idea and Reality* and *Literature and Psychology.*

A third book, growing out of a symposium on *Oral Literature and the Formula* in November 1974, is scheduled to appear in the spring of 1976, edited by Benjamin A. Stolz and Richard Shannon.

The present volume illustrates very well the special characteristics of the Center's conferences. They have regularly brought together scholars who had never met before—*would* never have met in the normal course of their scholarly lives—but nevertheless had significant insights, methods, questions, attitudes, to share with each other.

Unless I am much mistaken, readers of the book will be struck by at least two paradoxical features of this meeting of linguists and philologists: great diversity of linguistic material, from a span of several thousands of years, matched against community of problems and approaches; and obvious mastery of special disciplines and subject-matters combined with a desire to communicate across specialty boundaries and respect for the good will and intelligence of those on the other side. If the reader does perceive these paradoxes, he will have begun to share the exhilaration of the symposium itself.

Publication of these volumes has been made possible by a special gift to the Center by a resolutely anonymous donor.

A special word of thanks is due to Peg (Mrs. Herbert) Hayman for her superb typing, which has made this volume as well as its predecessor so attractive to the eye.

Gerald F. Else
Director

October 1975

INTRODUCTION

The idea for a conference devoted to the topic *Linguistics and Philology* (the order is alphabetical!) had a very modest origin about the year 1955. Shortly after I joined the faculty of the University of Michigan I met Herbert Youtie and we used to have long talks about various problems of 'reading' ancient texts; he would provide examples from Greek papyri, and I from various cuneiform languages. As we talked and compared and argued and considered the general problem of 'reading,' albeit by the modern reader-editor, we found that there were a great many common problems regardless of the language or the subject on which the text was written. There was a great deal of common sense (not common-sense), whether one came with a traditional philological approach or with a modern linguistics viewpoint. In fact, various underlying hypotheses and assumptions in each position had long been subconsciously integrated into the other. We both deplored the wide and widening gulf between the practitioners of the two arts, and the increasing abyss and divisions that had grown up among specialists in many language fields, with the result that Germanists, Classicists, Egyptologists, Assyriologists, and Sinologists had little to say to each other. There were but rare occasions when they might even have met in the same room. We therefore dreamed of an opportunity to have a very disparate set of language- and text-specialists meet together for a couple of days to see if there were any possibility of inter-field communication. Ever since those years in the middle and late 50s we tried to do something about arranging such a meeting, but for a variety of reasons our effort came to naught. So we let it lapse.

Then in 1971 Gerald Else distributed a note to many of us, asking for ideas for scholarly conferences that might be of interest to the Center for Coördination of Ancient and Modern Studies. The memo jogged my memory; Else reacted positively; and a committee consisting of Else, Marckwardt, Paper, and Youtie was formed and proceeded to look into the matter. The conference on *Language and Texts: The Nature of Linguistic Evidence,* held in

Ann Arbor on March 27-30, 1974, was the happy result; and this volume of the papers submitted for discussion at the conference is an attempt to provide a partial record of that meeting.

One basic question lay behind the planning for this conference: aside from the details of each language that make it a specialized subject impenetrable to the non-initiated, did there have to continue to exist a negative attraction or even antipathy between linguist and philologian? Surely the histories of the many fields of research into particular languages are replete with examples of scholars who combined an awareness of and delight in both approaches. Did the separation and divorce stem from differences of emphasis: classical versus non-classical languages, dead versus living languages, standard written versus regional dialect or non-standard languages? It is hardly necessary to be reminded that the non-classical, non-standard, non-ancient, non-literary fields all had to achieve validation before they were accorded status equal to the more traditional studies. We have seen time and again how data and principles from each end of the spectrum have illuminated and cross-fertilized each other.

Examples come to mind from several fields. The late distinguished American Sanskritist, Franklin Edgerton, made many significant contributions to a number of traditional problems of the Classical Sanskrit language and its rich literary tradition. But he also devoted many years of his life to the analysis of a dialect that bears the complex name 'Buddhist Hybrid Sanskrit.' I remember hearing him lecture on this subject on more than one occasion, and was impressed by his demonstration that many of the texts edited by serious and competent scholars had been incorrectly dealt with. Where the editors had noted numerous examples of 'scribal errors,' these were rather within the normal range of usage if one treated the particular texts from their own dialectal perspective rather than from that of an assumed dependence on the canons of another dialect, namely, the classical language. Others have spoken of Edgerton's feat as one of rescuing a language from the mistreatment of wrong-headed editors, and of having eliminated myriads of 'scribal errors' from the scholarly literature.

A second example I take, if I may be permitted to do so, from my own research into a language called 'Judeo-Persian,' i.e., Modern Persian written in the Hebrew alphabet. Here too scholars at the turn of the century availed themselves liberally of the 'scribal error' judgment when they encountered forms that did not conform to their notions of classical usage. In most cases, the forms which struck the editors as aberrant were in fact written confirmation of linguistic usages current in the spoken language. But scholarly attention had long been riveted exclusively on a written classical standard that was—as such standard languages often are—a highly artificial dialect based on historical norms quite out of touch with common colloquial practice. There was even very little interest in seeking information on the language as actually used. Concentration of effort solely on classical usage therefore served to produce almost total neglect of anything that did not fit the classical canon—to the detriment of meaningful investigation into the historical development of the Persian language from *all* pertinent data sources.

A third example may be drawn from Assyriology. Thirty years ago very few practitioners in that special field—I. J. Gelb was one of the few—insisted on the principle that one had to deal with each and every dialect of Akkadian (or Assyro-Babylonian) in its own terms, rather than on the assumption of a single Akkadian language with local deviation and aberrations in particular times and particular text-genres.

The papers in this collection draw on a wide variety of similar examples from a truly diverse range of language specialties. Thus we have here ample confirmation for the hypothesis that an occasional look outside one's particular field can be a fruitful and informative learning experience for every specialist. These contributions to the conference demonstrate over and over again the common heuristic methods of all textual study, despite the locally different emphases.

It was impossible to reproduce an edited version of the conversations and discussions that took place at the conference itself. That would have been a Herculean task. But the papers that were submitted in advance to all the participants served their purpose well and sparked a wide-ranging, exceedingly interesting series of talk-sessions—held without animus, with few axes to grind, and with a true sense of scholarly camaraderie that is rare even when specialists gather at their annual meetings. What remains most memorable, in my opinion, was the extraordinary nature of the event—carefully planned, to be sure—wherein a group of scholars representing such diverse specialties came face to face and found that they had matters of mutual interest to discuss. The likelihood that any three of them would ever have been in the same room at the same time (except for faculty meetings) was very remote; it was this that was unusual, instructive, and profitable. For a brief two and a half days we had taken a step toward the reëstablishment of a community of scholars. May there be more such efforts!

Most of the papers included in this volume stand very much as they were originally presented; only two or three were substantially revised. Professors Goldin and Marckwardt had an opportunity to rework the texts of their admirable—and relatively extemporaneous—statements. The task of editing these papers was a very gratifying one, for the essays read better a year later than they did when they were first submitted and discussed. I commend them to the reader with confidence that the particular combination of topics treated here will evoke the same kind of intellectual excitement that they produced in the conference participants.

It must be recorded, alas, that due to circumstances beyond anyone's control two of the planned participants were not present at the conference. Roy Miller was delayed at the last moment in returning from an assignment in Japan; and Herbert Youtie suffered a distressingly serious attack of influenza that made his presence impossible. Youtie's special role as godfather and planner has already been referred to and is here mentioned again with thanks.

Finally, a word of gratitude to Gerald Else for his magnificent support at every step of the way, which made the conference possible, and to his imaginative aid in furthering the publication of this volume; to Mrs. Evangeline Newton, who did all the detailed letter-writing, note-taking, and administrative back-up without which nothing could ever have happened; and to my wife, Bess, who is my best listener and encourager. And, of course, I cannot conclude without an expression of the most heartfelt appreciation to all who wrote these papers, and to the respondents, discussants, and other participants who made the conference so memorable.

Herbert H. Paper
Editor

May 1975

PROGRAM OF THE INTERDISCIPLINARY SYMPOSIUM

*LANGUAGE AND TEXTS: THE NATURE OF
LINGUISTIC EVIDENCE*

March 27-30, 1974

supported by a joint grant from the National Endowment for
the Humanities and the A. W. Mellon Foundation

Advisory Committee: Herbert H. Paper, Albert H. Marckwardt,
Herbert C. Youtie, Gerald F. Else.
Conference Coördinator: H. H. Paper

Public Lecture

Reinhold Merkelbach, University of Köln: "The Bey of Roses: A
Modern Turkish Tale and Its Roots in Ancient Ritual."

Session One

I. J. Gelb, University of Chicago: "Records, Writing, and Decipherment."

*Respondent: Herbert H. Paper
Departments of Linguistics & Near Eastern
Studies

James Barr, University of Manchester: "The Nature of Linguistic
Evidence in the Text of the Bible."

Respondent: Charles R. Krahmalkov
Department of Near Eastern Studies

Commentary: Gene Gragg, University of Chicago

Discussion

Session Two

D. R. Shackleton Bailey, University of Michigan: "Editing Ancient Texts."

> Respondent: Ernst Pulgram
> Departments of Romance Languages & Literatures & Classical Studies

Reinhold Merkelbach, University of Köln: "Greek Vocabulary and the Christians."

> Discussion

Session Three

Chaim Rabin, Hebrew University of Jerusalem: "The Classical in the Modern: A Study of Contemporary Hebrew Literary Language."

> Respondent: Gene M. Schramm
> Department of Near Eastern Studies

Morse Peckham, University of South Carolina: "Editing 19th Century Texts."

> Respondent: Robert H. Super
> Department of English Language & Literature

Commentary: John C. Gerber, University of Iowa

> Discussion

Session Four

Mary R. Haas, University of California at Berkeley: "Methodological Problems of American Indian Philology."

> Respondent: Kenneth Hill
> Department of Linguistics

Robert P. Austerlitz, Columbia University: "Literacy and Folk-lore—Philology and Linguistics: Sacred Eurasian Antiquity and Profane Worldwide Modernity."

Respondent: Gernot L. Windfuhr
                     Department of Near Eastern Studies

Discussion

Summary Commentary: Judah Goldin, University of Pennsylvania

Discussion

Summary Commentary: Albert Marckwardt, University of Michigan

Discussion

PARTICIPANTS IN THE SYMPOSIUM

Robert P. Austerlitz   Linguistics, Columbia University

David R. Shackleton Bailey   Classical Studies, University of Michigan and Harvard

James Barr   Near Eastern Studies, University of Manchester, England

Gerald F. Else   Classical Studies, University of Michigan

Ignace J. Gelb   Assyriology, University of Chicago

John C. Gerber   English, University of Iowa

Judah Goldin   Oriental Studies, University of Pennsylvania

Gene Gragg   Oriental Institute, University of Chicago

Mary R. Haas   Linguistics, University of California, Berkeley

*All respondents were University of Michigan faculty members.

Kenneth Hill	Linguistics, University of Michigan
Charles Krahmalkov	Near Eastern Languages & Literatures, University of Michigan
Albert H. Marckwardt †	English Language & Literature, University of Michigan
Reinhold Merkelbach	Classical Studies, University of Köln, Germany
Herbert H. Paper	Linguistics, University of Michigan
Morse Peckham	English, University of South Carolina
Ernst Pulgram	Romance Languages & Literatures, University of Michigan
Chaim Rabin	Hebrew Language, Hebrew University, Jerusalem, Israel
Gene Schramm	Near Eastern Languages & Literatures, University of Michigan
Robert Super	English Language & Literature, University of Michigan

LITERACY AND FOLKLORE–PHILOLOGY AND LINGUISTICS; *SACRED EURASIAN ANTIQUITY AND PROFANE WORLDWIDE MODERNITY*

Robert Austerlitz

LITERARY AND FOLKLORE–PHILOLOGY AND LINGUISTICS; *SACRED EURASIAN ANTIQUITY AND PROFANE WORLDWIDE MODERNITY*

Robert Austerlitz

Introduction.

The purpose of the cumbersome title is to compress a maximum load of information into it. The dichotomies in it are imperfect; their asymmetry is designed to stimulate discussion.

It took me a long time to understand exactly what is to be done at this conference. In order to gain such an understanding, I tried to extract the unifying idea of the conference from the titles of the papers as they were announced. Before going on to my own subject, I will therefore try to communicate briefly: (a) what my understanding of the structure and purpose of the conference is, and (b) a few comments which I thought deserved to be made in the course of this introduction.

As I see it, our area of inquiry is basically divided into societies which have a script and those which have no script: see nodes 1 and 2 in the rudimentary tree given below. The first of these either poses the problem of decipherment, 3 (Mr. Gelb's paper), or does not pose it, 4.

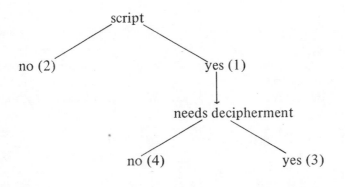

Branch 4 of the tree is its most complex one. I see it as requiring the following dimensions,

		ANCIENT	MODERN
SACRED		A	X
PROFANE	LITERARY	B	D
	NON-LITERARY	C	Y

i.e., ANCIENT vs. MODERN, SACRED vs. NON-SACRED (here: PROFANE); and within the last category, LITERARY vs. NON-LITERARY. In this matrix of six cells, four are occupied: A (Mr. Barr), B (Mr. Shackleton Bailey), C (Mr. Merkelbach), and D (Mr. Rabin). The two unoccupied cells, however, are no less deserving of inquiry. X, MODERN-and-SACRED texts do exist. Depending on our interpretation of what is sacred, they could range from the most recent translation of the Bible to cultic rock texts, among many other things. At the other end of this MODERN-and-SACRED pole (X) lies Y, NON-SACRED-and-NON-LITERARY-and-MODERN. This is the huge class of non-literary texts in our present-day life: it comprises the bulk of what is being printed today.

Our tree, as we have erected it so far, requires one more node, namely at point 2, where it bifurcates into the New World, 5 (Ms. Haas), and the Old World, 6 (Austerlitz). By fiat, both 5 and 6 are restricted historically to the modern period. The fact that there are written languages in the New World is distorted by me; see below.

Our full-fledged tree, then, looks like this:

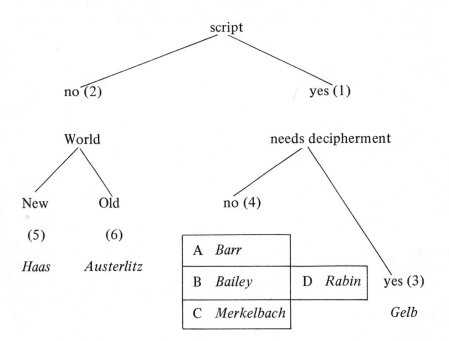

Having done our scheme one injustice already (in regard to script in the New World), let us do it another and assume that the tree could be optimally symmetrical. Such optimum symmetry would point up certain lacunae in it which may turn out to be instructive. The distinction between LITERARY and NON-LITERARY which plays a role under PROFANE at point 4 in the tree (see the matrix above) is, of course, not applicable to the category SACRED. Still, if LITERARY and NON-LITERARY are to be taken to mean, somewhat unimaginatively, 'written down' and 'not written down,' an interesting category could be introduced here, namely that of 'unwritten ritual texts.' These would be folkloristic ritual texts which, for some reason or another, are not (or are not allowed to be) written down in societies which have scripts. I do not know of any such texts but would be interested to hear from anyone who perhaps does. Branch 2 of the tree is also impoverished. Everyone knows, of course, that the New World, 5, also has scripts, both ancient and modern, so that the problem of decipherment, 3, also comes up in branch 5. A lacuna which deserves mention in passing, however, is the distinction

SACRED vs. PROFANE in pre-literate societies. In my own experience, based mainly on Gilyak (spoken in the Amur-Sakhalin area of the Far East), this distinction is a very important one: the vocabulary of the sacred is often quite different from every-day language and, presumably, often quite archaic. It is of great utility for the internal reconstruction of the language. It is, by the way, different in some regards from poetic language, which is also different from every-day language. Thus the dimensions we are talking about (still in connection with unwritten languages) yield the following categories:

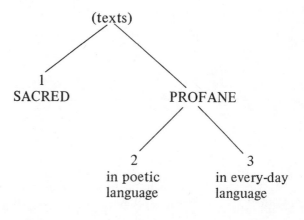

where 1 and 2 are, in fact, more closely related than the branches in the diagram would indicate. Students of style may, in fact, prefer a schema such as:

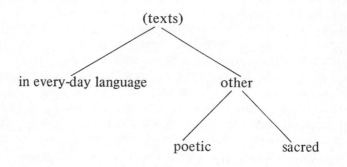

I. *Literature and Folklore.*

There seems to be some kind of tacit assumption or consensus that 'literacy' and 'folklore' describe a polar relationship. It is not altogether unjustified, because it is well known that a society with a high rate of literacy will, predictably, show a low incidence of concern for folklore; and, conversely, we know that folklore is often collected in societies which are deprived of the benefit of script. On closer inspection, however, I think that the tacit assumption is superficial and dangerously misleading. It seems to be based on a grid, itself incorrect, such as:

where the absence of a connecting line between 'illiteracy' and 'folklore' also marks the flaw. Obviously, societies with a literature may and generally do also have folklore; though it is true that illiterate societies (more aptly now called pre-literate) can have no written literature. This brings us to the problem of 'written' vs. 'oral' literature, which I would like to dispose of in part by saying that 'oral literature' is folklore but that 'written literature' is more than folklore which has been written down for posterity. I would like to broaden the concept of written literature at this point to include a conscious line of descent among authors and of literary genres. Thus I would like to think of (written) literature as consisting of traditions the bearers of which are aware of their roles. Furthermore, this class of persons (i.e., authors) gives rise to or requires another class of persons, the parasitic class of critics, who cannot exist without authors. (Sometimes the author and the critic are housed in the same person.) I would like to propose that the critic is a sub-species of the philologist: he tries to understand a text, an author, or a period through a close reading of that text, although his tools may be much less refined than those of the philologist-properly-speaking who is to be discussed in section II. The purpose of this point is to show to what degree the concept of 'philology' can be strained.

In the domain of folklore, the analogue of the author is, of course, the *Volksgeist*. What is the analogue of the critic? He has none in the society, unless it is the same *Volksgeist,* which guides and reshapes folklore in the course of time. But who analyzes folklore, with a view to understanding its author, a given folklore text, or a given period in folklore? It is the folklorist, who more often than not is not a member of that society (or who, even if he is, detaches himself from his own folklore for purposes of scientific objectivity) and whose methods are largely borrowed from other disciplines.

We have arrived at a minor paradox: *literature,* which owes its existence and survival in time to an artifact, *script,* generates the parasite (the critic-philologist) who is a member of the society which shelters that literature. Folklore, on the other hand, requires and has no artifacts for its survival in time; by the same token, it generates no parasites within the society which could be considered analogous to the critic-philologist. This minor paradox should bring out in relief the close, perhaps intimate, relationship which obtains existentially between the critic-philologist and his subject matter: he is or should simulate being a member of the society (linguistic community) in which his subject matter is embedded. The reason for this is that his subject matter consists of cultural values or other very human products which require inspection at an intimately close range. By contrast, the linguist can and often does look at the object of his inquiry from afar, as does the folklorist, for reasons dictated by scientific method or ultimate purpose (diachronic or transcultural comparison, global generalizations, or attempts at prediction motivated by theory).

II. *Philology and Linguistics.*

We can now continue to pursue our comparison of the roles of the philologist and linguist at closer range. For the philologist, language is the principal vehicle of culture, generally at a specific point in space and in time, e.g., the Middle Ages in Italy. He can study this vehicle in two ways: he can study the text (for it is almost always a running text) in and for itself, thus coming very close to the enterprise of the linguist; or he can study the meanings, covert and overt, in the text with a view to gaining an insight into the culture of the period. In the latter sense he is a cultural historian, one who is more intimately involved with a document than the average cultural historian (who synthesizes and then generalizes). For the linguist, language is an object which can be studied, as we know, in many ways. In the narrowest sense, the linguist is a grammarian (a technician versed in *technē grammatikē*) who analyzes either a text or artificially severed parts of texts, so-called paradigms. He can do this synchronically, for one period (one speaker, one document dating from a definite period) or dia-chronically, for successive periods; he can do it for an entire speech community or for speech communities in contact or at a remote distance from each other. What is more, he can try to un-cover generalizations about human behavior or the human mind in general (or, at the other end of the pole, he can totally eschew anything that smacks of value judgments, i.e., meaning). Rather than list all the possibilities called for at this point, I will only re-mind the reader of some of the most basic dichotomies in the study of language from the linguist's point of view—diachrony : synchrony; langue : parole; paradigm : syntagm; arbitrariness : (its opposite); form : meaning; substance : function; expression : con-tent; code : message; emic (distinctive) : etic (*in naturā*); acquisi-tion of language : loss thereof; etc. (In spite of this bias toward binarism, not everything needs to be stated in binary terms: the linguist is also concerned with change as such, with sounds as such, with degrees of tractability, with value or valence, etc.)

It is obvious from what I say here, I hope, that linguistics is much more ambitious than philology: by pre-empting all of lan-guage as its domain, it literally makes claims on all aspects of human life which can be communicated about in terms of lan-guage. It is this ambitiousness which places linguistics in positions adjacent to almost all forms of human inquiry—but which also makes it vulnerable: the adjacent areas are also colonial powers in their own right and conflicts are not infrequent. (At Yale, the De-partment of Linguistics is in the Faculty of Social Science; at Columbia, it is in the Faculty of Philosophy [i.e., the humanities]. Phonetics courses are notorious for being offered at teachers' col-leges for future speech and drama teachers, in the engineering school for acousticians, perhaps in the medical school for oto-laryngologists, in the anthropology department for prospective field workers, and sometimes in the linguistics department.) To return to vulnerability: we have seen in the last decade how much discussion generative grammar has generated in psychology, philosophy (particularly logic), statistics, sociology, not to speak of areas which are situated at the closer periphery of linguistics. Some of us are even embarrassed by the ambitious claims made by generative grammar: that it can hope to explain human behavior, that it can capture what is innate in the brain of the human species transculturally, that it can make generalizations inductively about all languages and thus zero in on universals of language. Generative grammar is not the only school to have made such ambitious claims, I think. H. Steinthal (1823-1899), for example, Wilhelm von Humboldt's best known and most productive student, seems to have thought that the study of language can answer questions in psychology, philosophy, and physical anthropology.

Having thus established that linguistics is much more imperialistic than philology, is there nothing analogous we can say about philology? There is. I am thinking of Karl Vossler, Erich Auerbach, and Leo Spitzer—all philologists of the first rank—who may not openly claim that by having studied a given body of texts they understand a period, but seem to me to imply that they do. (I am especially thinking of Vossler's statements on the Renaissance.) However, the analogy between linguistic and philological imperialism is forced and I do not want to push it too far. It is true that philologists, unless they are specialists in areas other than literature, may sometimes neglect the non-literary aspects of a period or of an author; but it is also true that their main concern, even if tacit, is either to trace our own descent from a previous period in history or to contrast such a period with our own (or with another period). The fact remains that philology has much more modest aims than linguistics; its profession of being an *ancilla* 'handmaiden' is justified and true.

Is there perhaps one sub-domain of linguistics which bears comparison with philology, as understood above? Yes. It comes from a surprising quarter but is, I think, worthy of being mentioned. It is the American notion of 'anthropological linguistics.' The anthropological linguist tries to gain access to the inner recesses of a culture through the study of the language of its speakers. His primary aim is to understand the speakers' values and the mode in which they communicate them. Studying this sort of behavior bears comparison with the philologist's concern with a text or body of texts. He too is concerned with uncovering the inner recesses of a culture or of a given aspect of such a culture. There are differences, but I think that they are not differences in kind. In theory, the anthropological linguist works with an open, endless corpus while the philologist by definition works with a closed corpus. But we know from experience that all open corpora are closed because of our human limitations in time and energy. A few other differences: the philologist is chronology-oriented; he is very much interested in predecessors and successors (of a text, an author, a form). This preoccupation with history is not anathema to the anthropological linguist, but more often than not he is not engaged by it because, while he is an anthropological linguist, he is still decoding the language. (Once he has decoded it he can go on to become a comparative ethnologist/ethnographer or, as he is more properly called, a cultural anthropologist.)

There are also a few more superficial aspects to this comparison between the role of the philologist and the anthropological linguist. The latter can ask an informant a question and can elicit an answer; i.e., he can ask the message-carrier a question about the code. The philologist can never do this; at best he can find a treatise contemporary with the document which he is studying about the subject which he is studying in the document; i.e., a text about a text. A text about a text is comparable to asking an informant a question about his language-and-culture and receiving a good answer.

In this section I have tried to show that philology and linguistics do not, strictly speaking, form a pair and much less a dichotomy. The aims of linguistics are much too broad to permit this. Conversely, the aims of philology are much clearer in themselves than those of linguistics and are much more clearly dovetailed into practice and theory in adjacent disciplines. Not completely whole-heartedly, I have proposed that the domain of the philologist is comparable or perhaps even analogous to that of the anthropological linguist.

III. *American Linguistics.*

Just as there is an anthropological linguist, there is an anthropological archaeologist whose analogue is the fine-arts archaeologist. At Columbia University, the archaeology of Mesoamerica and South America is offered in the Department of Anthropology (in addition to methods-and-theory and fieldwork courses), while the archaeology of the Bible, of Anatolia and Syria, of the Near East, and of pre-Islamic Iran is offered in the Department of Art History and Archaeology. This brings me to my last imperfect dichotomy, that of the prejudice we seem to harbor in considering Greek and Roman antiquity and the ancient Near East as somehow more dignified than the rest of the world. The more professional we wax, the more we admit India and China into the inner sanctum. The fact that American archaeology poses basically the same array of problems does not deter us from classing it, broadly speaking, with the sciences whose focus is more in the secular, contemporary world. The reasons for this are understandable and need not be given in great detail: Mediterranean and Near Eastern antiquity are more closely connected with our own religious, philosophical, and legal heritage and have an older history in our universities than the study of the past of other parts of the world; the focus of Amerindian studies has been ethnographic and ethnological (with linguistics in its train); our philological and cultural-historical equipment for the study of our own heritage is superior to that which is available for the study of the rest of the world—see the discussion in section I. These are not the points which I would like to discuss here. Rather, I would like to draw attention to the secular—if I may say so—nature of American linguistics after Whitney.

William Dwight Whitney (1827-1894) was a truly remarkable figure. He combined the highest competence of the 19th-century continental comparative linguist with the sovereign clear-headedness of 19th-century Anglo-American thinking. His influence in general linguistics is presumably superannuated now; but it is of interest to note that he lived at an age when the competent comparatist and philologist could coexist, in the same person, with the general linguist-theoretician. The next figure of Whitney's stature to appear on the scene after him was Franz Boas (1858-1942), who pulled the center of gravity of American linguistics away from traditional comparative work and philology and toward an interest in Amerindian languages. The early Boas was a physical anthropologist, the later Boas was also a social anthropologist; but his significance lies, among other things, in the large number of his students, among whom Edward Sapir (1884-1939) was the most outstanding. If the humanistic component in Boas was minimal, at least as far as I know, it played a large and important role in Sapir throughout his life: he wrote on Herder, on poetry and meter, and on music but did, as we know, magnificent work in Amerindian languages and in general linguistics. As in Whitney, the philologist and the theoretician-linguist coexisted in Sapir without stress. They also coexisted in Leonard Bloomfield (1887-1949); but it was in Bloomfield's time and largely through the exemplary exactitude of Bloomfield's own work (much of which was in Amerindian languages) that structuralism began to predominate in general linguistics as practised in the United States.

There is no inherent disagreement, as such, between the ethos of philology and structuralism; but the strong emphasis on descriptive linguistics (rather than comparative, which must always contain the elements of a historical orientation and hence an in-built sympathy for philology), a strong wind of positivism which blew over the continent and brought with it a mechanistic conception of the methodology of describing languages, and the slow attrition in teaching and learning classical languages—all conspired to unite Bloomfield's disciples in a camp which was inimical to a culture-bound view of language. It is important to note that Amerindian specialists were much less affected by this wave than others.

The enormous advantages of a strictly scientific method, as introduced into American structuralism, also strengthened the dogma that everything pre-structural was unscientific; and the ethnocentrism which was an heir to our exaggerated concern with our own sacred Eurasian antiquity became the object of ridicule. By thus cutting itself off from its humanistic heritage—which, to be sure, had often impeded the progress of the positivistic and mechanistic achievements which seemed phenomenal at the time— American linguistics of the 1940s also cut itself loose from the benefits of that heritage. Two examples should suffice here: (1) The description of a language was to take place step by step, and the anticipation of a subsequent higher step was to be avoided at all costs for fear of circularity. (2) Reference to meaning was to be avoided completely in phonology and was to be kept at a minimum in morphology because form was considered as being more tractable than meaning (as indeed it is). Point (1) disregarded the fact that, because of its complexity, language simply begs to be described with circularity in the investigator's mind. Point (2) inhibited the development of syntax.

I have overdramatized my account and neglected to stress strongly enough the fact that not all practitioners of linguistics

were equally (or at all) convinced of the benefits which would
accrue from this new methodology. But the schism was complete,
and profane modernity had established itself by 1956 when the
revolution came in the form of Noam Chomsky's then fresh
transformational grammar. In spite of some justified and some unjustified claims that generative grammar has pre-Neo-Bloomfieldian
roots (they have been traced to Humboldt, Descartes, the Port
Royal grammar, and Sanctius so far), the damage remains unre-
paired. In the meantime, education has also changed to the point
where reverence for the past—a natural, automatic, and highly
edifying by-product of a philological orientation—is no longer
taught and much less acknowledged in some quarters of the community of linguists.

It would be unfair to say, I think, that generative grammar
and philology cannot be reconciled. It would be more accurate to
say that the domain of generative grammar today (as distinct from
its earlier transformational progenitor), and especially its claims,
are so different from the concerns and claims of philology, that
there is hardly any intersection of the two left. As for linguistics
in general and *its* relationship with traditional philology, I refer
the reader to what was said in section II about the parallelism between philology and the anthropological linguist, especially the
Amerindianist in North America.

IV. The situation in Asia is somewhat different and is to a
large extent dependent on political realities. As I see it, we must
first of all distinguish on the one hand between countries with old
and high cultures, emerging nations, and Soviet Asia, and on the
other between cultures with an old native philology and those
lacking such an old native philology (let us call them 'tribal' for
the moment).

	Old & high-culture country			Emerging nation		Soviet Asia
Native Philol.	China	India	Japan	Thailand	Burma	Outer Mongolia
Tribal	Lolo	Toda	(Ainu)	Lahu	Karen	Kamchadal

The table given here should serve only as an example of the range of some of the possibilities which face us. China has an old tradition of native philology which is still part of the equipment of linguists in the 50-year-old bracket, even if they are trained in 20th-century methodologies. I have no information about the younger generation of linguists. The situation for the older ones is felicitous. Presumably, whatever work is to be done on tribal minority languages such as Lolo (which happens to have a native script but no native philology) will also be done by practitioners with both native and modern training. Ceylon and India have a wide array of native traditions living side by side; I know that work with tribal languages is in progress in the Dravidian area, where native Tamil linguists are working on Dravidian tribal languages (at Annamalai University). In spite of its exaggerated modernity, Japan is still faithful to its native traditions; although among linguists these seem to be receding in favor of the most recent Western ideologies. Nevertheless, Shirô Hattori and his students have salvaged Ainu materials in such large quantities, it is hoped that when in the near future the language is no longer spoken, Ainu philology will see the light of day. This would be a case of happy collaboration between the linguist (at present, as collector) and the philologist (in the future, as the beneficiary). Thailand, Burma, and Vietnam each has its own native traditions, but these are less tightly organized around institutions than the corresponding traditions in China, India, and Japan. These countries are also blessed with large numbers of tribal languages, related and unrelated to the national language, which require investigation. There are still too few native specialists in linguistics and much of the work is still being done by foreigners (some of whom have excellent training in the native philologies). I know of only very few native linguists in Indonesia who also have traditional philological training (e.g., in Javanese), and I know nothing about any work on tribal languages. In the Republic of the Philippines, the accent is on tribal languages. I have no information on Cambodia, Laos, Nepal, or Tibet.

This is a very superficial listing of what seems to be the situation in the old cultures and in some of the emerging nations of Asia, taken as representative types.

The U.S.S.R. presents a similar picture, with one or two added complications. All of Siberia is part, administratively, of the

R.S.F.S.R. 'Russian Federation.' This means that all of the
minorities in Siberia are in contact with the Russian language and
with Russian culture and that most of them have been in contact
with the Russians since the opening of Siberia. Though such contact with Western culture goes back two or more centuries, it is
not spread out evenly—a fact which contributes to the complexity
of the situation. Furthermore, since 1917 the Soviet regime has
launched very energetic literacy campaigns, both in the local (tribal or larger) languages and in Russian. These have been quite successful; but since the U.S.S.R. is in the grips of urbanization and
industrialization, it is not difficult to imagine the existential
quandary of the semi-educated or educated non-Russian Siberian.
This situation spills over into the realm of higher learning as well.
The fine tradition of linguistics in Imperial Russia was first continued in the Soviet Union, then abruptly interrupted by Marxism,
and finally reinstated under Stalin. Currently the trend is to emu-
late the West (or to outdo it). Where does this leave linguistics in
its relation to philology? See section II. What I say here applies to
Siberia, but the Islamic peoples of Soviet Asia present a still more
complex picture. Some of these have a native philological tradition
and some do not. Those which do are fettered by the dominating
atheistic ethos which inhibits native philology. The Caucasus presents still another picture: Georgia is bubbling with activity in all
quarters; presumably there are also native Georgian specialists in
other Mingrelian languages. There are no clear indications from
Armenia, however. Work is being done in the tribal languages of
the Caucasus, presumably also by natives. All in all, the situation
in Soviet Asia is more encouraging because (1) traditional schools,
if any, have been slower to atrophy, in spite of some strong
counter-forces which would, one thinks, encourage extinction, and
(2) the anti-humanistic currents in some species of Western linguistics have not reached the U.S.S.R., yet.

    I will not discuss the Near East because there are too many
experts present among the participants. Still, a word needs to be
said about Turkey. Could it be that the now discredited *güneş dil
teorisi* 'theory of the sun-language' is still inhibiting progress in
both linguistics and philology in Turkey? Here is a country in
which the two could truly fertilize each other.

V. *Conclusion.*

I admit that section IV is very sketchy. It is so cursory because a great amount of detailed work and observation would be needed to gauge the situation thoroughly and correctly, and because of the incompatibility which is inherent in the linguistics-vs.-philology dichotomy, as I hope to have shown elsewhere in this paper. This basic incompatibility is exacerbated, in the case of modern Asia, by all the vigorous trends which can be subsumed under modernization. In the last analysis, the answers to the most important questions about language lie outside linguistics, in this case in the sociology of the future.

Given all the factors enumerated for Asia above, we may project a time in the future when the smaller tribal languages will have become extinct, but when their memory, in the shape of data competently gathered by trained native linguists and ethnographers, will survive. That will be the time when the philologist will be able to embark on husbanding and processing the well-preserved surviving corpus with a view to reconstructing the lost culture. To anticipate the trend, I reproduce in translation a short Gilyak tale (also found elsewhere in Northern Asia) which I collected from my informant in the 1950s:

> Once upon a time, the Proto-Gilyak, after having received a writing system from the gods, were travelling from one place to another by rowboat. A very heavy rain came, so heavy that they and all of their belongings got completely wet. They therefore landed and unloaded everything, spreading it on the ground to dry. They also spread out their script (presumably on paper). But a very strong wind came and blew their sheets of paper away. That is why the Gilyak have no writing system.

EDITING ANCIENT TEXTS

David R. Shackleton Bailey

EDITING ANCIENT TEXTS

David R. Shackleton Bailey

The editor of a text in a language which has long since passed out of general currency faces linguistic and other problems which vary enormously from one given situation to another. There are, after all, a vast number of ancient languages, more or less preserved through written materials. There is at one extreme, for example, the case of Etruscan. It seems that according to orthodox opinion, unconvinced by Zacharie Mayani's diagnosis of this mysterious tongue as an early form of Albanian, it has no traceable affinities elsewhere, and the materials for studying it are too scanty to offer much hope of progress. The meanings of a number of words and inflections are established; speculation and ingenuity may get further, hardly much further. But at least the script is intelligible. On the other hand, the student (or editor) of Mycenaean Greek has to cope with a complex and not yet fully deciphered script and a similar shortage of materials; but if the basic premise of the Ventris-Chadwick decipherment is correct, as now seems to be all but universally acknowledged, knowledge of later Greek can be used to elucidate this ancestor. The editor of Vedic hymns is in business on a larger scale. His materials are literary and exist in respectable quantity. The stages of development from Vedic into classical Sanskrit and thence to the languages of modern India can be traced in detail. The Vedic editor has to use and evaluate a long tradition of interpretation by Indian pundits, naturally following principles different from those of modern philology. The language is fairly well known, but particular words and phrases, even whole stanzas and hymns, remain enigmatic. As one editor wrote, the dark places are very dark. Light reaches some of them from the science of comparative linguistics. The meaning of dubious words can be revealed by cognates in other Indo-European languages, especially the sister language of ancient Persia, Avestan.

Probably no man has known more about the Indo-European linguistic family than my famous namesake Sir Harold Bailey (once my teacher and colleague). With awe rather than fascination

(for this approach to languages has never greatly appealed to me),
I used to watch him rapidly covering sheet after sheet of 'Cambridge scribbling paper' with Avestan, Greek, Hittite, Old Irish,
Ossetic, and so on (not forgetting, of course, their putative progenitor, Indo-European), to illustrate a Sanskrit word. He himself gave
a new member to the group by resuscitating the language of Kho-
tan in Central Asia. Khotanese Buddhist texts were unravelled and
edited by Bailey with the aid of comparative linguistics and of
parallel writings in known languages. Lacking experience in this
field I speak vaguely. Has anyone written on the application of
comparative technique to the elucidation of languages unknown or
partially unknown? Perhaps like many tricks of the editor's trade,
it is all a matter of practice, hardly reducible to general formulae.

Buddhism, like Manicheism, covers a multitude of languages:
Sanskrit, Tibetan, Pali, Mongolian, Chinese, Japanese, to mention
only the most important. I used to be much concerned with the
first two, where one finds a peculiar situation, perhaps unique.
Apart from the Pali texts of the *Little Vehicle,* the voluminous
Buddhist scriptures and still more voluminous ancillary writings
(comparable to the products of Scholasticism in mediaeval Europe)
were mostly composed in Sanskrit, or in the 'hybrid Buddhist
Sanskrit' on which Franklin Edgerton became the world's leading
authority. The conversion of Tibet to Buddhism virtually began in
the seventh century A.D., and in the course of the following centuries entailed the translation of innumerable works of this character from Sanskrit into Tibetan. These two languages are utterly
dissimilar, Tibetan belonging to the Sino-Tibetan family, with
Burmese as its closest important relative. Moreover, the activity
began before Tibetan became a literary language (the script now in
use is an adaptation of the Indian *devanāgarī*). How then to transfer doctrinal works from a complex and sophisticated language,
with a highly developed specialized terminology, into one of totally different structure in which no corresponding terms and concepts existed? Flights of lamas traversed the Himalayas to spend
the best part of their lives in the great Buddhist monasteries of
India, studying language and lore. Then they set to work. It was
often impossible for them to produce accurate renderings which
would be fully intelligible apart from the original, so an elaborate
system of linguistic convention was evolved. Sanskrit words and
constructions were given standard Tibetan substitutes, embodied
in lexica; and no matter how widely the sense of the Sanskrit

expression might vary, the substitute, which would carry no corresponding semantic range in its indigenous usage, would do its regular duty. To give an easy example, Sanskrit verbs (like Greek or German) are frequently compounded with prepositional prefixes modifying in various ways and degrees the meaning of the simple verb. Tibetan verbs did not do this. So conventional equivalents for these prefixes were produced and regularly used, irrespective of the actual semantic function of the prefix in each case. The Sanskrit prefix *pari* (Greek *peri*) meaning 'around' or 'wholly' becomes *yoṅs su* ('wholly'). But the compounds in which *yoṅs su* plus the Tibetan 'equivalent' of the simple Sanskrit verb yields in normal usage a sense corresponding to the Sanskrit compound are a minority. Tibetan versions, therefore, have to be understood, often can only be understood, in the light of the original.

This is a generalized account. Translators varied, as did the nature of their texts. Sometimes, especially in dealing with elaborate poetry in the classical Sanskrit style, the Tibetans were hopelessly at sea; usually they could follow fairly well the sense and structure of their original. But the results, if I am not much mistaken, would often be as dark to Tibetan readers, especially those not trained in the same discipline, as they are apt to be to European scholars when the Sanskrit text is lacking, especially to those who have not acquired long familiarity with the conventions employed. But where the Sanskrit texts exist in a corrupted form, these conscientious, not to say mechanical, versions are of great assistance to their editors.

My efforts in this direction were largely spent on two songs of praise to the Buddha, generally known as the Hymns of 150 Verses and 400 Verses, respectively, composed by one Mātrceṭa in the first or second century A.D. They were without doubt the most celebrated Buddhist hymns ever written, once sung, as we are told, in every Buddhist monastery; but after the downfall of the religion in India the Sanskrit text disappeared. Some fragments turned up in China and were published early in this century. Then in 1936 an Indian scholar found a complete manuscript of the shorter hymn in the library of a Tibetan monastery, which he transcribed on the spot and then published. But the text was still in a deplorable condition, due to corruptions in the manuscript and no doubt to errors on the part of the transcriber. To reform it, I was able to procure photographs of a number of manuscript fragments hitherto unpublished. To these materials were added an eleventh-century Tibetan translation (in three slightly variant versions), a ninth(?)-century commentary originally in Sanskrit but surviving only in Tibetan, a seventh-century Chinese translation, and, for good measure, a short fragment of yet another translation into Kuchean, a language of which I have never known a word.

The Chinese rendering, the work of a famous Buddhist author and savant called I-Tsing, is a complete contrast to the Tibetan in translation-technique. I-Tsing's method resembled Ezra Pound's. Apparently he took some sort of mental impression from the original, and then produced a stanza of his own which might be a loose paraphrase or an almost independent product, starting from some word or phrase in the Sanskrit which had happened to catch his attention. I-Tsing's literary merits have been praised by Sinologues, but like Pound he must have been a better poet than linguist. His performance was of no great help for my purposes and it was a question whether or not to include it in the edition, particularly as my knowledge of Chinese was at that time inadequate (it is now non-existent). Finally I let it in, mainly because such polyglot editions are useful to students of the languages and translation-techniques involved.

Combination of these categories of evidence made it possible to form a text which, I think, left practically no unsolved problems. In problems of interpretation the commentary helped, but being a Tibetan translation its meaning was sometimes in doubt (*obscurum per obscurius*), and even when clear was not to be followed uncritically. In syntax, morphology, and metre, Mātṛceta conforms closely to classical norms, but his vocabulary and allusions are distinctively Buddhist. Obviously the more an editor of such a work knows of classical Sanskrit as well as of Buddhist literature, thought, and terminology, the better equipped he is to tackle its special difficulties.

The longer hymn, of 400 verses, offered another kind of challenge. It survives in a number of fragmentary manuscripts (housed in the Berlin Academy of Sciences) in a difficult north-Indian script sometimes called Slanting Gupta, quite different from *devanāgarī*—fortunately the photographs made available to me contained a romanized transliteration by a great expert, Wilhelm Siegling. A large part of the text thus survived, interrupted by fissures and chasms, ranging from single missing syllables or parts of syllables to blocks of half a dozen stanzas or more. So far described, the situation was pretty much that presented by a fragmentary Greek papyrus. The important difference lay in the existence once again of a Tibetan translation (but no commentary, and, happily, no Chinese). Part of this had been published many years previously by a former Professor of Sanskrit at Oxford, F. W. Thomas, with his own English translation. The latter, when compared with Mātṛceṭa's Sanskrit, proved to be a cautionary example of the dangers of such an undertaking, for which Thomas's attainments in Tibetan were insufficient anyhow.

The reconstruction of the text was an engrossing task. Work on the shorter humn had given me some familiarity with Mātṛceṭa's style, though this longer one is more complex and artificial, full of the verbal ingenuities in which classical Sanskrit poets delighted. For example, one section of the hymn consists of puns, in which Brahminical terms are given Buddhist applications (another is devoted to praise of the Buddha's *membrum virile!*). The filling of the smaller lacunae was generally safe and easy. As for the larger ones, all depended of course on how clearly the Sanskrit showed through its Tibetan disguise. I suppose that even the best of Latinists, if he had to construct a couple of lines of Virgil from one or two words with a modern verse translation to assist, would not have much prospect of restoring them verbatim. But with due attention to the technique of Tibetan translators this could sometimes be achieved with a high degree of probability in Mātṛceṭa's case, so at least it seemed to me. If ever a complete manuscript turns up, we shall see what we shall see.

Before moving elsewhere let me notice another problem which often plagues the editor of an Indian text, though it did not arise with Mātṛceṭa. Ancient India was notoriously lacking in historical sense, insofar as that consists in a desire to fix past events in their context of time and place. Literary products, especially when their purpose was not primarily literary, were often treated as adaptable and expendable—the great Mahābhārata epic is mostly superstructure. Doctrinal works were particularly liable to pious accretion, nor was abridgement forbidden. Faced with a collection of manuscripts each representing the same but different book, the plight of an editor is unenviable.

If I asked a specialist in Hittite or Icelandic how far editorial situations in his field resemble those above described, I should be prepared to be told that differences outweighed similarities. But of the whole company, classical Greek and Latin must stand conspicuously apart, simply because of the amount of editorial and other effort which has been applied to these two literatures and to the studies connected with them. The apparatus at the editor's disposal, such as dictionaries, grammars, concordances, treatises beyond count on every conceivable special branch of classical enquiry, far exceeds anything comparable elsewhere. He will find himself at the end of a long chain of predecessors reaching back to an *editor princeps* soon after the invention of printing in Europe, to say nothing of usually anonymous laborers in the Middle Ages or in antiquity itself. This does not mean that he will find nothing fresh to contribute, but that his techniques will be more sophisticated and controlled, as those of a surgeon in a modern operating theatre. And much of his work will lie in the evaluation of earlier work. The reviewer of a recent edition of Heraclitus observes that "the reader is frequently informed that a scholar is wrong without being told what his view is. M.'s discerning knowledge of a mob of more than two hundred modern interpreters is outstanding and admirable. It is a pity, however, that this vast knowledge was not displayed with greater clarity of principle and that the ringleaders were not separated more often from the rest of the mob for as much as perfunctory debate."

It is generally recognized that a classical editor's first duty is to furnish the best possible text. Professor Dodds of Oxford, himself a highly accomplished textual critic, once opined that our (classical) texts are good enough to live with. I suppose that depends in the first place on one's standard of living. Certainly a great deal has been done for nearly all of them (much more for some than for others); a good modern text compared with a sixteenth-century one will show that on every page. But not all modern texts are good. Many are produced by editors badly trained and badly equipped, conservative because the evidence of their manuscripts is the only evidence they think they understand, who not only fail to push back the frontiers of darkness but revel in it as their natural environment. The same issue of the *American Journal of Philology* from which I have just quoted has a notice by its editor concerning a book on Statius's *Silvae*. Professor Luck writes: "The recent Teubner text is hardly better than one of the 15th-century MSS . . . it is a sobering experience to discover how utterly unreliable our current texts are . . . very often the true reading was discovered centuries ago and then forgotten." Let us hope that a few competent practitioners and a larger number of instructed readers will continue to keep the new barbarians at bay.

The task is many-sided. Since the texts of a classical author will be based upon manuscripts ultimately deriving from his original draft, the editor must trace the history of its transmission and establish the relationships of the surviving copies so far as that can be done and has not already been done to his full satisfaction by predecessors. Thus a mob of manuscripts can become a family or even, should it turn out that one is the direct ancestor of all the others, an individual. The techniques of 'recension' have been intensively studied as well as applied since Lachmann edited Lucretius in 1850, and in many cases there may not be much for a newcomer to add in this direction. Important new evidence is hard to come by, though a new look at old evidence can sometimes be unexpectedly rewarding. It has to be acknowledged that this kind of research can take up a great deal of an editor's time without contributing appreciably to its legitimate purpose of improving a text (I say 'legitimate' because I doubt if anyone would admit to pursuing it for its own sake).

Then there is palaeography—the study of scripts and the habits of copyists. Scribes, as Housman said, will write anything for anything; but usually a scribal error has an assignable cause, often visual, as the misreading of a letter or combination of letters—though psychological factors too are frequently present. Manuscript authority is all too often treated as an absolute: in each case, you take it or you leave it. Really it is a variable, not only because some manuscripts are less trustworthy than others, but also because some errors are so easy and common that an editor who understands his business will feel quite free to postulate them whenever other evidence points that way. For example, the not very common Roman name Publilius is constantly changed by copyists to the common forename Publius—the converse change naturally hardly ever occurs. The editor who emends *publius* to *publilius* is not in any significant sense defying manuscript authority (which, of course, is often necessarily or legitimately defied even when it really exists).

One fallacy recalls another. An editor's choice of reading should depend on a balancing of evidence, which may be complex and multifarious. But the degree to which an emendation changes the sense of the passage in question is not evidential. For instance, the insertion or excision of a negative will usually turn the sense upside down and hence is sometimes regarded as a 'violent' procedure. R. Y. Tyrrell wrote in 1891: "It ought to be regarded as the last resource of despair, in criticism, to change the quality of a proposition by the insertion or omission of *non*. Any expedient is better than this; yet editors often resort to it"—as did Tyrrell himself on occasion. His contemporary, J. S. Reid, knew better: "The circumstance that *non* is not in the MSS has little weight if any. In his note, Müller gives a number of examples and his list might be increased indefinitely." A textual change which ignores palaeographical probability is a violent change in the only proper application of the term. When Moriz Haupt said that, if his reason required him to substitute *o* for *Constantinopolitanus* (or was it the other way round?), he would follow reason—that was an illustration. It would be a violent proceeding, whether it materially changed the sense or not, because it postulates an error which no copyist would be likely to commit. Equally, a palaeographically easy change loses nothing in plausibility by its semantic impact.

Often, however, the choice of a reading, whether from among manuscript variants or by way of conjecture, is to be determined by criteria of intrinsic probability—what Bentley called *ratio et res ipsa*—sometimes even against the authority of manuscripts and the indications of palaeography. Intrinsic probability may have to do with a fact. When manuscripts make an author state what is wrong in fact, ignorance and deliberate falsification being ruled out, the editor has to choose between convicting him of a slip or changing the text. In one of his private letters Cicero refers to the section on jokes in his dialogue 'On the Orator,' written a few years earlier, as having been put into the mouth of Marcus Antonius, who is actually one of the two main speakers in the dialogue; but this particular section is given to a minor character, Caesar Strabo. Editors generally, and I think rightly, hold that Cicero's memory could have played him false here and that the name in the manuscripts should stand. If Cicero had revised his letters for publication such a mistake would be much harder to condone. The text of another letter refers to Themistocles's exile *and return*; but as a matter of generally accepted historical fact Themistocles did not return from exile. Here there are three lines of defense. Cicero's memory is again at fault, or he is following a variant historical tradition, or he is referring to the return of Themistocles's bones for burial. The third suggestion, in the context, is a mere absurdity. The second has been supported by a passage of Aristotle which on more careful inspection turns out to be a broken reed. And even if the existence of a variant tradition could be established, Cicero would not have dragged it in here. So we are left with lapse of memory. But this was a very carefully written letter of which Cicero was proud, and the lapse would have been quite extraordinarily unfortunate in that the letter is addressed to a historian whom he wanted to write a monograph of *his* Consulship and exile and return. The conclusion seems inescapable that this is a case of textual error. There is no certain restoration; perhaps *interituque* 'death' for *redituque* 'return' is the best of several suggested. Factual evidence naturally looms large when we are dealing with expository works involving technicalities, as of philosophy or astrology or medicine; as indeed it does in these same letters of Cicero, which teem with references to contemporary persons and affairs. Lacking specialized knowledge of these, even the genius of a Madvig was severely handicapped.

Manuscripts sometimes present statements at odds with their context, or contrary to the author's known opinion or sentiment, or redundant, or nonsensical. The question then is whether the author's performance in general is such that the fault can credibly be attributed to him rather than to a copyist. Allowance has to be made for such things as poetic license, hasty composition, logical failure, and temporary insanity. But there are limits.

In poetry, and sometimes even in prose, metre and rhythm provide criteria. An editor who happens to be English and over fifty will probably have absorbed the more salient rules of Greek and Latin poetic metres early in life through the now moribund practice of verse composition. But there are refinements which only reveal themselves to close analysis, and each poet has his own practice. Research on prose rhythms has been going on for almost a century. This too can help textually, though the rules are more elastic and much remains in dispute.

The majority of textual problems raise questions of language—style, vocabulary, syntax, grammar, morphology. Since knowledge of these matters has to be drawn almost entirely from the surviving specimens of Greek and Latin literature, the textual (no less than the literary) critic must never forget how much has *not* survived.

We possess 44, or maybe 43, plays by the four great Athenian dramatists of the fifth century B.C.; between three and four hundred of their plays were extant in antiquity and thousands more by other playwrights. Only a very little of all this has come down in papyri, anthologies, and scattered quotations. Ovid, again, in one of his latest poems mentions about thirty contemporary versifiers. One of them has left us a few hundred lines, a few others some short fragments, but most are now only names.

Mediaeval copyists produced countless solecisms, most of which were corrected once and for all in the sixteenth century or earlier. The modern editor cannot expect to find such easy employment. But he will often be called upon to pass judgement on expressions which do not seem conformable to the usage of the author or his period. Given the limitations of our evidence the absence of a parallel is not necessarily significant; but an inexplicable desertion of a well-established norm is fairly suspect. Did Cicero ever use the preposition *versus* without another preposition (*in* or *ad*), except with the names of towns and small islands, as later writers very occasionally did? Can he be allowed to write *Tarso Amanum versus* 'from Tarsus to (Mt.) Amanus' or has *ad* or *in* dropped out? Cicero uses the preposition *versus* so seldom that we cannot be sure that his practice might not have varied. But he uses the verb *adipisci* 'to gain' scores of times. In two passages editors print it in the form *apisci,* common in earlier Latin, but in only one[1] (in a letter) is there manuscript warrant for doing so. In that one, on any reasonable estimate, a copyist is more likely to have written *api-* for *adipi-* than Cicero to have causelessly departed from his otherwise invariable usage. On the other hand, the old form is unobjectionable in a letter of his correspondent Servius Sulpicius, who had a jurist's partiality for the archaic.

An unparalleled usage may, however, be justified by analogy. I cannot do better than quote a paragraph from Housman's review

---

[1] The other is *Laws* I, 52 on which the latest commentary (1971) has this to say: 'For *ascindi* (BH; om.A) Feldhügel [1852] reads *adipiscerdi*. . . . A better reading is *a[pi] scendi* since *apisci* also occurs elsewhere in Cicero's writings and is closer to BH . . . cf. *Fam.* 4, 5, 6, *Att.* 8.14.3.' *Fam.* 4, 5 was not written by Cicero, and the palaeographical evidence in favor of *apisci* is a trifle (the copyist could omit the four letters almost, if not quite, as easily as the two); the linguistic evidence against it is powerful. Why then do editors go on printing it? For the reason implied in F.R.D. Goodyear's remark that 'happily there are even today a few critics for whom *ratio et res ipsa centum editoribus potiores sunt.*'

of Palmer's *Heroides:*[2] 'vi. 3 sq. hoc tamen ipsum debueram scripto certior esse tuo. Palmer writes *debuerat . . . certius,* because he says *hoc certior esse* for *hoc scire* is not Latin. Not so fast: that no example of this construction has been adduced is true . . . but what is unique is not therefore wrong, and the next step is to look for examples of analogous constructions. These are forthcoming: just as the accusative of a neuter pronoun stands here with *certior sum = scio,* so does it stand with *auctor sum = suadeo* in Cic. Att. XIII 40 2 'quid mihi auctor es?' and fam. VI. 8 2 'quid sim tibi auctor?' Therefore I call it more likely that Ovid made *certior esse* govern *hoc* than that Ovid's scribes turned *debuerat certius* into *debueram certior.*"

A non-specialist who opens a classical commentary and finds that much of it consists in quotations from Greek and Latin authors may harbor a suspicion that they are really there to display the editor's learning; and sometimes the suspicion might not be entirely misplaced. Properly chosen parallels do, however, illuminate and attest as nothing else can. What Greek and Roman writers could or could not write has to be determined on the evidence of what they actually did write. Walter Headlam's procedure when he settled down to edit Herondas can still be recommended. Let the editor master his text, observing all peculiarities and doubts, until his mind has grown a set of antennae sensitive to any conceivably helpful radiation from outside; and then let him read and read. Great repositories like the *Thesaurus Linguae Latinae*[3] will supplement this work, but they do not make it superfluous. As Housman put it, "a scholar who means to build himself a monument must spend much of his life in acquiring knowledge which for its own sake is not worth having and in reading books which do not in themselves deserve to be read."

Many classical editions, like the Teubner and Oxford Classical Text series, offer only texts with a selection of variant manuscript readings and conjectures. The production of a full verbal commentary should not involve any important extension of an editor's scope, since textual decisions are largely interpretative. How should a scholar detect and remove corruptions in a text which he cannot understand? A great many supposedly corrupt passages

---

[2]*Classical Papers,* p. 473.
[3]This mammoth was born in 1900 and is still only half grown. The earliest volumes desperately need revision.

have finally been vindicated by intelligent and informed interpreters.

It is often open to editors, and may even sometimes seem
obligatory, to go far beyond these limits in order to handle historical or legal or archaeological or other problems for their own
sake and not merely so far as may be necessary to make an author
intelligible. Usually, though, such independent work is better presented as a separate treatise, and I suppose the same holds good
for literary criticism, which calls for faculties quite other than
those that go to make a commentary. Most of the large output of
such work at the present time does in fact take the form of special
books and articles. Not that literary and verbal criticism have
nothing at all to say to one another. The latter often demands
literary taste and a sense of style. The former, not underpinned
by accurate verbal scholarship, may be seen bombinating in the
void.

> sunt hic etiam sua praemia laudi,
> sunt lacrimae rerum et mentem mortalia tangunt.

There are no more familiar lines in the *Aeneid* and none more
often misunderstood. Innumerable readers, including Matthew
Arnold, and some editors have taken *lacrimae rerum* as 'tears *of*
(or in) things' instead of 'tears *for* things'; which latter meaning is
plainly demanded by the context and attested by a closely parallel
expression (*lacrimas Creusae* 'tears for Creusa') elsewhere in the
poem. Jackson Knight, in his book *Roman Virgil,* has it both
ways: "which seems to mean in prose not much less than, 'There
is no denying that even in this far-off land honour gets its due, and
they can weep at human tragedy; the world has tears as a constitu-
ent part of it, and so have our own lives, hopeless and weary; and
the thought that things have death in them breaks our hearts and
wills and clouds our vision.' " Then on for a page and a half. One
need not be hard on Jackson Knight for making an old mistake,
due to inattention as much as to ignorance, and I am not about to
quote worse examples from more recent publications. It would not
be difficult, but this is not a pillory. Nor do I imply that the 'higher' interpretation of classical writers is to be discouraged even in
their editors; only that Greek and Latin are best either learned or
left alone.

THE NATURE OF LINGUISTIC EVIDENCE
IN THE TEXT OF THE BIBLE

James Barr

THE NATURE OF LINGUISTIC EVIDENCE
IN THE TEXT OF THE BIBLE

James Barr

1. *General.*

When we ask what is the nature of linguistic evidence, one may well follow up with the further question: as evidence of what? The answer may divide our subject into two or three aspects. First, we may consider linguistic evidence in a text as evidence of the language itself: how far does the text give accurate evidence of the language in which it was written? As we shall see, this is certainly a moot question in the case of biblical Hebrew. Second, we may consider linguistic evidence as a guide towards the interpretation of the text itself; no doubt this is a moot question with any text. There is a third category: one might consider linguistic evidence as evidence of the extra-textual and extra-linguistic circumstances, e.g., in attempting to use linguistic evidence to trace historical folk-migrations or social changes. In this paper I shall have the first two kinds of question mainly in mind.

This paper will be devoted for the most part to the Hebrew Bible (Old Testament, in Christian parlance); the problems of the New Testament may be expected to overlap somewhat with those of classical Greek and Latin texts, and therefore only limited attention will be given to it—in particular to its background in the Semitic language world.

A. *The Hebrew Bible.*

2. *The writing system of the Hebrew Bible.*

The text of a Hebrew Bible, as presently printed, can be said to include two components, and these can be distinguished both historically and functionally. I shall refer to these as the 'base text' and the 'pointing'; it is customary to designate them as the consonantal text and the vocalization, but this designation is a loose one, as we shall see. In traditional style we might illustrate as follows: the base text is a linear string of characters, e.g., *mlk*; the pointing is a series of points or marks, added above or below the consonants; and thus our group *mlk,* when supplied with the marks for -*e-e-,* would be read as *melek* 'king,' and if supplied with the marks for -*ā-a-* would be read as *mālak* 'he reigned.' Thus the text can be thought of as comprising three bands or tracks: the central one carries the base text, and the upper and lower carry the pointing. The reading of such a text involves a number of rules by which the reader correctly combines information from the two components in the right order so as to form a linear sequence of consonants and vowels.

There is general awareness, however, that Hebrew has not always used this two-component script: in fact the second component, the pointing, was added to the Bible text during the period about 600-1000 A.D.; before that time the text was written in a one-component (traditionally: 'consonantal') form only. Moreover, such one-component (unpointed) writing continues to be widespread and indeed is normal in Hebrew except for such special cases as the printed Bible.

The traditional distinction between a 'consonantal text' and a 'vocalization,' though roughly tolerable in practice, is inexact. On the one hand, the base text includes the marking of some vowels. By use of the system of *matres lectionis* or vowel letters certain characters, which otherwise stand for consonants (mainly *h, w* and *v*), are used to mark vowels. Such marking of vowels is, however, (a) in some degree optional and variable, and (b) in some degree ambiguous (thus *w* can stand for either *o* or *u, y* for either *e* or *i,* etc.). But, subject to these limitations, some marking of vowels takes place throughout the base text: perhaps, very roughly speaking, something like 20% of vowels are so marked, and conversely perhaps 20% of the 'consonants' written (i.e., of the characters of the base text) stand in fact for vowels. Thus the base text is consonantal not in the sense that each character written stands in fact for a consonant in the text as spoken, but in the sense that the base text includes only characters from the inventory of those that *may* be used to stand for consonants and indeed commonly do. Conversely, no sign in the second component, the pointing, ever stands for a consonant.

Again, just as the unpointed base text normally marks some of the vowels, so also the pointing, though often called the 'vocalization,' includes some consonantal information which would otherwise not be furnished. The most important such information is the marking of long consonants (gemination, Hebr. *daghesh*); this is phonemic and important, but is not registered in unpointed writing. To this we must add the distinction between the two sibilants *ś* and *š*, which in the base text appear in the identical graphic shape; and some other minor matters.

Moreover, the pointing of the biblical text includes not only vowels but also a further set of points, more or less one for each word, which are called the 'accents' and combine two functions: (a) a sort of suprasegmental musical-phonetic function, for guidance in the synagogue cantillation; (b) a function closer to that of our punctuation. In this latter function, the accents mark linkages between the elements of a phrase, and the boundaries between one phrase and another; all verses are divided somewhat hierarchically into larger and smaller segments by this means. Moreover, there is a certain linkage between the accents and the vowels in certain positions, a word that is accentually at the end of a major phrase having a different vowel pattern from that which it would have in another position.

3. *Procedures in reading.*[1]

The reading of Hebrew texts may proceed in several ways, and three models may be considered:

a. With a fully pointed text, there is a notation for each phoneme, and, apart from marginal cases, the two components can be and are blended by the rules of reading so as to provide a full linear sequence of phonemic text. (The basic rule is simple: you read the first sign in the base text [i.e., the first consonant], then you follow with the vowel indicated in the pointing, then you pass on to the next sign in the base text, and so on: in other words, the system works because syllables are taken to begin with

---

[1] This section follows an article by the writer entitled "Reading a Script without Vowels," now in course of publication in the Mont Follick Lecture series (Manchester University Press).

a consonant, though certain other constraints on syllable-forma-
tion exist). But what is important is this: the passage from the
written text to the spoken sequence is independent of semantic
understanding, or prior to it; thus a nonsense sentence can be read
aloud from pointed text.

b. An unpointed (one-component) text is read in a different
way. The text furnishes not a full linear series of signs for the
phonemes but a series with many gaps in it, each such gap containing a vowel. The gaps can be filled in *only if the reader comprehends the meaning of the text.* Thus in this case, semantic comprehension must precede the spoken realization of the text; and a
nonsense sentence cannot be phonetically read, or at best can only
be guessed at. The process of reading unpointed text is one of
rapid scanning in which the reader, from clues of various types
scattered through a sentence or phrase, comprehends the meaning
of the whole and thereby is able to supply the unmarked vowels
and associated information. The clues include: (a) morphological
patterns of words: many Hebrew words are of certain recurring
patterns which facilitate recognition; (b) syntactic clues: colloca-
tional relationships with other words reduce ambiguity and aid
identification; (c) semantic clues: semantic relationships with
nearby words also aid recognition, though far from infallibly. The
process of reading unpointed text is fast and familiar, provided
that the text is of familiar content.

c. The reading of a traditional religious text like the Bible is
a special case. As we have seen, the Bible was long transmitted in
unpointed form, and unpointed biblical texts are still in use for
certain purposes. But here we have to bear in mind the importance of the tradition of oral reading. The Bible was and is read by
trained reciters who have read it many times before. Though the
text was physically unpointed, the process is not the same as that
of reading an unfamiliar text such as a newly-arrived letter. In the
biblical case the reader works from two sources: (a) the written
text (unpointed); (b) his memory of the tradition of reading. Our
model (b) above may still be operative in part, but it is cut across
by another operation, namely the functioning of the base text as a
sort of mnemonic for the realization of the full phonemic sequence, which in principle derives from memory.

These three models will be of some help for certain historical
questions which will appear shortly.

4. *Basic historical data.*

Basic dates are somewhat as follows. The main body of the Old Testament was composed during the period 1000-400 B.C., but some very early parts date from before 1000 and some parts from after 400. Some, especially in the earlier period, may have remained in oral tradition for a considerable time before being committed to writing; but the exact interval is not known.

The main mass of manuscripts in existence, especially before recent finds, dates from 1000-1500 A.D. The pointed MSS from which modern critical editions are made date from about 900-1050 A.D. From this time and later, the MSS show a very high degree of uniformity except in matters of rather small detail; and forms of text with wide and major variations appear to have gone out of existence. With the Dead Sea Scrolls we have for the first time obtained some written texts from about 150 B.C.-150 A.D., but these as yet cover only a small portion of the Bible (the fullest coverage of a major book is Isaiah); these texts are of course unpointed. The evidence of the Dead Sea Scrolls suggests that at about the beginning of the Christian Era a text quite similar to the base component of our traditional text already existed, but that substantially differing text forms also existed.

5. *The nature of Massoretic activity.*

The first obvious problem lies in the wide discrepancy between the two components of the traditional text in respect of their historical origin. If the pointing was added in 600-1000 A.D. to a base text which in essentials had been so since 150 B.C.-150 A.D. (or even earlier), it would seem, at least at first sight, that two diachronically different states of the language had been compounded to form one text.

But this statement of the problem is a superficial one, for it takes as its defining point what is only the *graphic marking* of the pointing. The fact that these marks were added during 600-1000 A.D. does not in itself determine whether the linguistic features which they marked were old or were innovations of some kind. Here we have a division between two or more possible views of the work of the Massoretes, the scholars who developed the pointing systems and applied them to the base text. One view of their activity is essentially phonetically-based: There was an oral tradition of reading, handed down from one generation to another. Or, very likely, there were several such traditions, but one was considered to be superior. The Massoretes analysed this tradition of reading and registered it by a marking system, which started out in a simpler way and gradually became more complete and precise. More than one such system was in fact tried, and these different systems were related to different traditions: e.g., the Babylonian system differed not only in graphic form but also in structure; but in the end the Tiberian system, developed in Tiberias, more or less superseded others. In this view, the date of the graphic registration of the points does not tell us anything about the time of origin of the reading tradition that was registered.

Some scholars seem however to hold or to imply an exegetical-semantic view: the Massoretes studied the text, seeking an interpretation, and they provided the pointing, i.e., the second component of the text, according to the meaning that they thought right. If this view is followed, the work of the Massoretes must be considered more innovative in character.

It would also be possible to hold a mixed view and believe that the Massoretes generally worked in one way but occasionally, or in certain respects, in the other. I myself believe that the first view is the essentially correct one and that the Massoretes were in essence phonetic conservators rather than interpretative innovators;[2] but I would leave room for the possibility that in certain places and aspects they took decisions on semantic-exegetical or other grounds. And, since they took the existing base text to be in principle unchallengeable, they may in deciding between one reading tradition and another have been much influenced by the degree of coincidence between various reading traditions on the one hand and the details of the base text on the other.

But, even if the Massoretes worked on the graphic registration of an older reading tradition, we still have a probable large gap between the two components of the text; but that gap is to be measured not by the date of the final graphic fixation of the

---

[2] Cf. the argument of my *Comparative Philology and the Text of the Old Testament* (Oxford, 1968), chapter VIII.

pointing, rather by the origin of the reading tradition which was later thus fixed.

6. *Some possible historical reconstructions.*

Some parts of the Hebrew Bible were probably at first transmitted in oral tradition, in which case the original text was a phonetic text; only later was it written down. It would depend on the circumstances whether after the registration in writing, which extracts from the full phonetic text those phonemes which are relevant for the writing system, an oral tradition carried on a reading tradition of the whole (i.e., a tradition including the component not registered in writing). Some other parts were written from the beginning; if their circulation was in writing only, then readers would interpret them through a scanning for the semantic comprehension (model b in 3, above). Of some portions we have traditions that a text, long lost, was discovered and then read (Josiah's find of a law-book in the Temple); if this were true, then there would certainly be no reading tradition accompanying the written text.

An important part in comprehension was played by the changes in orthographic convention. We have seen that the base text registered some vowels, though ambiguously, through the system of vowel letters; and these vowel letters play an important part in the comprehension and oral realization of unpointed text, because they are a main source of the pattern clues (above, 3 b (a)): if the reader knows, even with some degree of ambiguity, one vowel within a word pattern, this greatly increases his ability to recognize the whole and thereby to identify the other vowels and elements not marked in the base text.

But the use of this mechanism depends considerably on being at home in the convention in use of vowel letters which is followed by the scribe whose text is being read. There has in fact been considerable variation in the use of vowel letters during the history of Hebrew. If they were used sparingly in early times, the use of them increased in the central period, and there was a great increase in the later period, as seen in various Dead Sea Scroll documents. Clearly, at least some circles considered it legitimate to rewrite the base text according to one's own conventions. But

Rabbinic scholarship, probably in the period 1-200 A.D., sought to revise and fix the written form of the base text, and in this went back to a less prolific use of vowel letters. This revision was, in its results upon posterity, successful in largely eliminating the deviant text-forms and establishing the basically uniform base text transmitted to the Massoretes and to later generations.

These orthographic shifts must in the later period be taken in conjunction with shifts in the structure of the religion itself. In the earlier and productive stage of Old Testament literature, the concept of a 'holy scripture' was at most embryonic, and no clear definition of the status of the material, and least of all of its details and its text, existed; some of the material now included in the Hebrew Bible may not have been thought of as particularly sacred literature, and even in concepts such as 'the law of Moses' the stress was on the content rather than on the detail of the text. In the Persian and Greek periods we have a crystallization of the material into a sort of canon of scripture; but this period also included, in all probability, notably in the early Hellenistic period, an element of what would later have been seen as considerable religious laxity. The later Greco-Roman period sees a great increase in literalism of interpretation, and a religious structure very strongly concentrated upon the Holy Scripture, especially the Pentateuch. This strictness of emphasis upon the Holy Scripture and the exact letter of it is the religious side of the movement which so greatly narrowed down the variety of textual traditions in the first two centuries A.D.

It would be a plausible reconstruction that the base component of the traditional text, selected and approved over others during 1-200 A.D., rests fundamentally on a text form of about 400-200 B.C., and that the reading tradition followed by the Massoretes has developed from one existing in 1-200 A.D., though doubtless having a history back even before that time. Thus the base text, once fixed in its orthography, would not alter; but the reading tradition would be subject to phonetic change.

It is reasonable to suppose that wide variations in the base text, implying error and corruption of that text, belonged to an early rather than a late stage in the development. Some portion of this variation goes back to orthographic differences: archaic orthographies might lead to misunderstanding of the text, and it was still permissible to rewrite the text in one's own orthographic fashion. But many corruptions cannot be explained through shifts in orthography, and depend on more fundamental errors in transmission. Some semantic rewriting of texts took place, in order to restate in 'modern' language what was understood to be the meaning; but on the other hand it is probable that many phrases which were unintelligible or barely intelligible were not rewritten but were transmitted as they were, for what they were worth. As we have seen, such semantically opaque phrases, transmitted in the base text, can be realized phonetically only by guesswork or on the basis of a reading tradition; in any case, such obscurities generally in due course generated an exegetical interpretation. In other cases, readings produced by errors in the transmission of the base text can be seen to have generated the oral readings (and, later, the registrations in points) which is natural to them.[3] Thus the process may have included a mixture of different procedures of reading, and the final Massoretic text as a whole probably includes a mixture of elements from different sources and periods, a mixture upon which a certain measure of standardization has been imposed. But the relation between the two components of the text is not rightly stated when one points simply to the dates when the base text was fixed and the pointing was added; the mutual involvement of the two components is both earlier and more complicated.

7. Changes in the social position of Hebrew.

Language change within Hebrew over the thousand years or so up to the work of the Massoretes would naturally be expected to have been great. But the matter is complicated by the shift in the social position of Hebrew. Within the period 400 B.C.-200 A.D., Hebrew gradually ceased to be the normal daily language of Jewish communities and came to be largely reserved for use as the language of liturgy and religious literature. Languages like Aramaic and Greek became the normal speech of large numbers, and both

---

[3]Thus in the parallel texts Ps. xviii.11/II Sam. xxii.11 the correct reading is *wyd'* as in the Psalm; in the tradition of Sam., the word was written as *wyr'*. This reading then generated the vocalization appropriate to it: *wayyĕrā'* 'and he appeared,' as against the original *wayyēde'* 'and he swooped.' The confusion between *d* and *r* was an extremely common source of error.

of these languages had a strong place within Palestine itself. The date at which Hebrew fell into complete desuetude even within Palestine has often been set too early, and it is a reasonable estimate that only the second great war against the Romans (132-5 A.D.) introduced the final stage of its decline. Moreover, Hebrew in the period (say) 100 B.C.-200 A.D. is known in a new form, called Mishnaic Hebrew (as the language of the legal discussions known as the Mishnah, completed about 200 A.D.) and different in many ways from biblical Hebrew. Aramaic, unlike Greek, was a Semitic language with many fairly obvious relationships to Hebrew, and it not only figures as a vernacular but gained a place within the biblical text itself, as the language of some chapters in Ezra and Daniel testifies. The marginal notes, written by the Massoretes in their work on the biblical text, are in Aramaic. And by the time of the later Massoretes, Arabic had become the dominant language of the Near East and was widely spoken by Jews. The introduction of points to the base text of the Bible had its parallels in similar activities vis-à-vis the Arabic Qur'an and the writing of Christian Syriac. Some scholars have thought that the development of grammatical theory had some influence on the procedures of the Massoretes. The relatedness of three great languages of Jewish life, Hebrew, Aramaic and Arabic, lent a comparative aspect to grammatical knowledge.

Did the fact that the normal daily language was other than Hebrew cause an accelerated distortion in the language of the biblical text? Or, conversely, did the fact that Hebrew was no longer in daily use enable the tradition of it to be preserved in a form purer than that which could have been attained by a language still under the pressure of daily use? Both possibilities have to be weighed. Perhaps one of them prevailed at one time, the other at another. It was, we may surmise, while Hebrew was still a language of daily use that it was most affected by Aramaic; the recognition of biblical Hebrew as a separate and special language, distinct not only from other languages like Aramaic but also from other stages of the same language, like Mishnaic Hebrew, tended to fix and to preserve its form.

8. *Types of questions involving linguistic change.*

It may be useful here to distinguish some different sorts of questions involved in the relation between linguistic change in

Hebrew and the status of the biblical text. First, some questions relate to historical phonetics: how did diachronic change affect the sounds of Hebrew, and what stage or stages of the process are reflected in the biblical text with its two distinct components? Second, some questions affect the central system of the grammar: what can be said about changes in the system as a whole, for instance in the morphology and the syntax, and how far may such changes have affected the evidential value of the text? Third, there are essentially semantic questions: what effect has the change of meanings, especially lexical meanings, had upon the status of the text as evidence? Some illustrations of these questions will be given in the following paragraphs.

9. *The text and historical phonetics.*

The written text of the Bible, even when pointed, does not in itself communicate to the reader what it sounded like when spoken, nor even what it should sound like when spoken today. The characters and points can be related to actual sound only through a factor external to the text, namely the existence of an oral tradition of pronunciation. The ancient speaker knew this because it was his language: for him, competence in the language included and presupposed competence in the phonetics, which he gained from his surrounding society and which to him was antecedent to his ability to read the script. The modern learner of Hebrew analogously learns the 'pronunciation' from his teachers. That the analogy, though real, is not total is symbolized by the term 'pronunciation': for this implies, as has been the historical fact, that the latter process begins from the script, the characters and signs of which the learner learns to realize in oral speech. But in either case the fact remains that the text itself does not 'give' us the phonetic realization of the language, and that this must be learned from a socially-given tradition.

There are in fact a number of indigenous Jewish traditions of pronunciation, of which the best-known are labelled (simplifying to some extent a distribution which is in fact more complicated) the Ashkenazi and the Sephardi (from north and east Europe, and from the Mediterranean and Levantine area, respectively).[4]

---

[4] For a recent survey, see S. Morag's article "Pronunciations of Hebrew," in the *Encyclopaedia Judaica* (Jerusalem, 1971), XIII, 1120-45.

Another important pronunciation tradition was the Yemenite. But most or all of these pronunciations fail in a greater or lesser extent to agree with the precise set of distinctions used in the marking of the biblical text. This has evoked in western universities the use of a more 'scientific' pronunciation, supposed to reproduce more of the distinctions implied by the writing system; its phonetics, however, are often wonderfully like those of English (or French, German, etc.) with a few exotic sounds added, mainly drawn from Arabic. This problem is of course analogous to that of the pronunciation of Latin or Greek in modern universities.

Of the differences between the pronunciation traditions of different Jewish communities, some probably go back to ancient times; but considerable elements appear to have developed in parallel with the phenomena of the vernacular dialects spoken (e.g., Yiddish, Ladino, Arabic). Such assimilation however is not total: the Yemenites, for instance, use in their reading of biblical Hebrew certain phones which are non-existent in their own Arabic vernacular, and they have separate traditions for their reading of the Hebrew Bible and for their reading of post-biblical Hebrew texts.

Something can be done to approach the ancient pronunciation through other channels. From Greco-Roman times we have a fairly large corpus of material transcribed from Hebrew into Greek or Latin scripts, including many proper names, and from this certain conclusions about the sounds of Hebrew at the relevant times can be reached. But the evidence has to be used with caution, for all of it is filtered through the phonemic and graphic systems of Greek and Latin, which had no resources for the marking of many distinctions essential to Hebrew.[5] Another possible recourse is to comparative linguistics, in that the sounds of a cognate language like Arabic may furnish suggestions towards the sounds of Hebrew; this approach is helpful but must be used with caution, and it is limited because many major Semitic languages of antiquity have died out without leaving any sort of pronunciation tradition (e.g., Akkadian, Ugaritic). Another source to which scholars turn in this connection is the pronunciation of Hebrew by the small separate sect of the Samaritans.

[5] For one instance, see the writer's papers "St. Jerome's Appreciation of Hebrew," *Bulletin of the John Rylands Library* 49 (1966-7) 281-302, and "St. Jerome and the Sounds of Hebrew," *Journal of Semitic Studies* 12 (1967) 1-36.

An illustration of this sort of question can be given from the laryngals, a group of consonants within Hebrew, which are all marked by characters in the base text. The Samaritans, however, realized these as zero, or in traditional terms 'did not pronounce them'; this fact, along with evidence from the Greek and Latin transcriptions, was long used in an argument that the Jewish pronunciation also had lost the laryngals but that these were 'restored' by the Massoretes. Though this case may be a false one (I doubt if the Greek and Latin evidence proves this), it may well have had validity for certain Jewish pronunciations; and in any case the idea that the Massoretes had a certain purist and restorative aspect in their work has to be kept in mind.

We thus see that the written text required to be supplemented by a tradition of pronunciation, and that many such traditions existed. It is an interesting question, how far the Massoretic notation was built upon one single pronunciation tradition than existing, and how far it included within the one system of notation features from different traditions then existing, so that the system is heterogeneous in its origins. But we may then ask whether this diversity of pronunciation traditions in the end makes much difference to the character of the text as linguistic evidence. Though the traditions are different, all of them can be related to this same text—only the paths between text and phonetic realization are different: the signs that will be realized as [t] and as [a] in one tradition will perhaps be realized as [s] and as [o] in another. Any one reading tradition is related to the text by a fairly simple set of links. Fundamentally this is because the pronunciation tradition is not related to the text itself in all its fullness and variety but only to its phonological system, its limited set of discrete and recurring consonants and vowels.

10. *The text and the grammatical system.*

Although the grammar of Hebrew is likely to have changed considerably during the course of the biblical period, the extent to which the text itself displays this is limited. The basic grammar, especially the morphology, of the Bible in its existing text is fairly uniform. What we find in very early sources are many anomalies and individually peculiar forms; but it could hardly be said that we find solid and substantial blocks of grammatical differences, such as we would find in (say) Homer and Euripides over a similar period of time. That the tradition should have levelled the grammar is not very surprising, since such levelling would favor intelligibility in later times. And yet the extent of this levelling should not be exaggerated: when we come down, let us say, to the post-biblical stage, with its form of spoken Hebrew known to us as Mishnaic and having some striking divergences from biblical grammar, there is little plausibility in any theory that biblical grammar was ever levelled to a Mishnaic standard. It is probable that the morphology and syntax of the main part of the Bible quite well reflect the situation of the central biblical period (say, 850-500 B.C.). What is really early and what is really late form two separate cases. Where texts involved really old stages of the grammar (say, before 1000 B.C.), either much may have been corrected into later forms, or some may have puzzled the later correctors too much, so that the old forms were retained but now formed something of a foreign body within the later grammar. Their retention might have to cause an anomaly or distortion on the phonemic/phonetic level. The case of late texts is different. These have certain new idioms differing from the usage of the central period (examples in Ecclesiastes, Esther, Chronicles, Daniel); but though these differ from the central period they fit with the language of the final stages and do not create severe comprehension problems.

Two examples from the verb system can be offered as illustrations:

Many scholars believe that Hebrew had a verb form ('passive *qal*') like *yutan* 'he will be given,' *luqah* 'he was taken.' But the forms were rare, and eventually they were reclassified as forms from other passive types; this in its turn had effects on the reading tradition and later the pointing. Actually, this example, though a good illustration of how the reclassification of forms could take place, is not tied to an extremely early date.

Second, a very characteristic feature of biblical Hebrew is the '*waw*-consecutive,' a system which depends essentially on the juxtaposition of 'and' to the verb. Working with two tenses, imperfect and perfect (so-called; and I use the term 'tense' in a completely empty sense, to designate a morphological category in verbs, with no implications about the function), we have this situation:

'and' + *verb* in one tense is transformed, if something is put between 'and' and the *verb,* into 'and' + x + *verb* in the other tense.

Thus if we take 'and he said,' and apply a simple negative transformation, we have:

$$\text{'and'} + V^{impf} \longrightarrow \text{'and'} + \text{'not'} + V^{perf.}$$

There is much dispute about how this little system arose, but no question that this is how it works. There is also no doubt that it eventually disappeared; it was still there in the 'biblicizing' language of some Dead Sea Scrolls, but was gone in Mishnaic Hebrew, for practical purposes. The signs of its passing are already visible within the biblical text in a quite considerable number of "exceptional" cases, within books like Kings, in which the older pattern is still generally regnant. In a book like Ecclesiastes, on the other hand, the 'new' situation, in which the system as outlined has broken down, is dominant. Thus in this case it is quite wrong to think that the grammar is levelled out throughout the entire Bible. But the 'old' situation was clearly the predominant one in most of the Bible; the 'new' can be accommodated without difficulty because it fits with the situation at the end of the biblical period. But it should be observed that the change of situation, as depicted above, does not involve the introduction of any new *forms*; it means rather that certain combinations of forms, which once had one function, now have another.

On the whole, one is inclined to suppose, in summing up, that the degree of levelling that has taken place in morphology and syntax is not very great and can easily be exaggerated; it would be most likely in extremely early materials which might have been inherited with important systemic differences, e.g., short vowels indicating case endings in nouns. In such cases the levelling was probably not done at the end of the biblical period, but rather at an early stage, in the assimilation of the material into a stage where the language system was different.

11. *The text and lexical and semantic problems.*

These have been particularly prominent in recent scholarship. The hypothesis widely implied is this: many Hebrew words or elements suffered misidentification in the course of transmission of the text. Either the meanings were forgotten altogether, so that at a later time meanings had to be obtained by guesswork, or else the meaning of a word was mistakenly understood to be that of another word. The restoration of the (hypothetically) correct meaning can be described as semantic emendation. Just as, in the familiar procedure of textual emendation, it is presumed that the text has been corrupted and a better original text is suggested by the scholar, so in semantic emendation the text (or at least the base text) is left untouched but a quite different semantic effect is reconstructed for this same text. The source from which new semantic identifications are gained lies to a very limited extent in other stages of Hebrew or in extra-biblical Hebrew inscriptions (which are very small in extent); to an immensely greater extent it lies in suggestions gained by comparative linguistics from cognate languages such as Akkadian, Ugaritic and Arabic. A form being known in one of these languages, and this form having elements (usually, consonants) which stand in relations of regular correspondence with those of the Hebrew text, and the meaning of this form in the other language being known, a meaning akin to it is now deduced for the Hebrew form and that meaning is now taken to replace the meaning previously believed to attach to the Hebrew form. Though this meaning is more or less novel to the understanding of meanings for this Hebrew word, it is claimed that it should now replace the meaning previously accepted. Large numbers of suggestions of this type have been made in modern scholarship, particularly by a few very active individuals; if even 25% of them were accepted, it would mean a considerable reconstruction of the network of Hebrew semantics.[6]

It is not my purpose to discuss the degree of validity of this method of reconstruction here; suffice it to recognize that the method exists and has been widely practised. What arises from it, and what it illustrates that is significant for our purpose, is the fact that the text in itself does not, strictly speaking, communicate meanings to us. The text communicates meanings only when it is read in conjunction with a competence in the semantic comprehension of the Hebrew language; or so it seems. This competence was acquired by the ancient speaker in the social process of his

---

[6]The entire method involved in these suggestions is investigated by the present writer in his *Comparative Philology and the Text of the Old Testament* (Oxford, 1968).

acquiring the language; and it is acquired by the modern scholar in his learning also. Given an adequate competence of this sort, there is a process of interchange between the knowledge of meanings stored from previous experience and the facts of the text. The situation is somewhat parallel to that we found in relations between the text, taken as phonemic/phonetic evidence, and the traditions of pronunciation. But there we were dealing with elements of limited number and very frequent recurrence (the vowels and consonants of the language, and the signs marking them). The process of semantic emendation has been most densely applied to elements which are rare or isolated, in some cases unique, within the biblical text. The Bible contains quite a large number of such words, and in many cases the interpretation of them has been long recognized as difficult, because of the lack of evidence beyond very few instances. The Bible is a very limited corpus of text to represent the totality of ancient Hebrew literature, and inscriptions and such extra-literary discoveries have added only a tiny amount more in Hebrew from within biblical times. Yet, though semantic emendation has affected the words which are acknowledgedly very rare and isolated (because their form is found only once or twice), it has more typically begun to identify, within the group of forms assigned to one word with a known meaning, cases which are now said to belong to a word identified from outside Hebrew, which word has come within the history of the text to be confused with a word more traditionally known. Moreover, though the method often appeals in its own justification to the existence of rare and isolated forms, it has come increasingly to affect the meanings attached to even commonly recurrent words such as prepositions.

We have seen that the text does not in an absolute sense communicate basic meanings; but, given a basic network of meaning, the text through its interrelations communicates a great deal *more* meaning. Given the present propensity to semantic emendation of Hebrew language elements, the importance of the text would seem to be that it provides the essential check against all such suggestions, against which they have to be measured. The new meanings suggested depend basically on a cross-language comparative operation, normally within Semitic languages; but the test of them must be whether they are required by, and supported by, the syntactic relationships of the text within Hebrew. Once again, the points at which semantic obscurities occur in the text and at which scholars have undertaken semantic emendation of meanings are clustered on the whole in the older segments of text and in the poetical sections, the diction of which is often unusual and poorly paralleled.

And, finally, whatever the future judgement of scholarship upon the present trend in semantic emendation may be, it should be reiterated that the core of biblical Hebrew consists of a vocabulary which is well evidenced by repeated use and of which the meanings can be thoroughly checked and known. The scholar, though he may start from the tradition of meanings in its modern form, as embodied in modern scientific dictionaries and similar works, will go on from this to see how the meanings emerge from the text and are refined and more fully defined by it.

12. *The text and poetic form.*

This is one of the weak points in the biblical text: it is ill-adapted to the display of the poetic form. Though the 'accent' marks (para. 2, p. 3, above) are in a sense poetic or musical and relate to the cantillation of the text, their value for the original poetic form is limited, for: (a) scholars do not generally believe that they represent the original poetic form; (b) the accent marks are applied in the same way whether the material is prose or poetry. There is indeed a somewhat different system of accents used in three books (Psalms, Job and Proverbs), which in this respect are sometimes called 'the poetical books,' but this does not really alter the argument.

Thus the text does not set out any identification of the poetic form except for a limited setting out of the material in lines (modern critical editions will set out in lines the poetic sections found in, say Genesis or Isaiah, but this appears to rest only on the editor's own authority), and basic knowledge of poetic form depends on scholarly theories of what the principles of prosody were. All scholars attach a heavy influence to parallelism ('Who shall go up into the hill of the Lord / and who shall stand in his holy place?'); but other theories have approached the subject from a more metrical viewpoint, seeking to identify numbers of stresses, of syllables, etc., which counted in the metre. A 'lamentation' type with a 3 - 2 line (number of stresses) is one of the types most widely agreed on. Another possibility is a principle more syntactic in character: the poetic form depends on a variety of syntactic line-types, which can be formally analysed (e.g., $NP^1 + V - NP^1 + V$).[7]

If the metre depends on numbers of stresses, syllables, etc., it is again likely that through processes of language change the metre of the oldest portions of the Bible will have become most submerged.

13. *The ancient biblical translations.*

As we have seen, the Hebrew Bible came down to posterity in a very uniform state of text, compared with other ancient literatures such as the Greek and Roman classics or the New Testament. There is however another line of evidence. After 300 B.C. the Bible was translated into Greek, the text basically and roughly called the Septuagint. Other translations into Greek, into Latin and other languages followed later; but the Septuagint (LXX) is for our purpose the most important in many ways. Used with due knowledge and caution, it may give access to a state of the Hebrew text, and to a network of Hebrew meanings, at a time lying before our earliest manuscript evidence in Hebrew (the Dead Sea Scrolls), and vastly antedating the pointed mediaeval manuscripts. The basic question in interpreting the evidence of the Greek text is usually this: does the Greek rendering give evidence of an original Hebrew which differs from the Hebrew already attested to us? Or does it give evidence of a mode of understanding by which the Greek translator interpreted a Hebrew text that was much the same as ours? And, if the latter, is it an understanding that was then current among Hebrew speakers, or is it one generated in his mind by the special (and in that age unprecedented) task of translating such materials into Greek?

The Septuagint came down to us by a different line of transmission: while the Hebrew text was transmitted within Judaism, that of the Septuagint was transmitted within Christianity. Nevertheless attempts were made to correct the Greek text on the basis of the Hebrew; but in spite of this the general conditions of transmission were quite different. The Latin Vulgate of Jerome (about

---

[7]This line of study is now being pursued by Mr. Terence Collins at Manchester.

400 A.D.) is significant because of his contacts with Jewish language and interpretation at that time.

Finally, not a translation, but a separate text tradition within Hebrew itself: the Pentateuch of the Samaritans. Their distinctive tradition of Hebrew pronunciation has already been mentioned; their text also shows some important variations.

Sources of this kind, by being derived from the tradition of the Hebrew text and/or the reading of it at some early stage, may when used with proper care be found to give testimony of variant forms and traditions which fell out of existence in the Jewish tradition when it was narrowed down to a more uniform and canonical form.

14. *Principles of text-editing.*

In general, editors of modern critical editions of the Hebrew Bible have not set themselves the aim of printing the text as (say) Isaiah wrote it, or even the text as it was when all the books were complete. Rather, editors have aimed to print the 'Massoretic text,' i.e., the complete pointed text as it emerged from the Massoretic process. Indeed, many printed editions have taken it as their aim to follow the first printed texts of the Renaissance period. More recently, editors have moved from this aim to that of printing as their text the text of one of the great manuscripts which emerged at the first perfection of Massoretic activity, the Leningrad Codex (1008 A.D.) or the Aleppo Codex (10th century).

It might appear that editing of the text of the Hebrew Bible has had something of the schizophrenic about it. In printing the text the aim has been the faithful reproduction of the Massoretic original taken as model; in the apparatus (or apparatuses, since the kinds of evidence may have to be separated out) the editor betrays his awareness that the text he has printed may be very remote from that which was written by the biblical writer, or from that which was current at the end of the biblical period. Here he adds variant readings that may have been suggested by the Septuagint, by the Samaritan, or simply by the ingenuity of modern scholars. Might it not therefore be better to seek to print the text that the editor thinks is the farthest back that the evidence can reach? It might some day be possible, if enough Dead Sea Scrolls were discovered to cover the entire Bible, to print an edition based on such a text. But no such edition is likely ever to take the place of a Massoretic edition: partly of course for religious reasons, but also for reasons which follow from the argument of this paper—the text was transmitted in two components, and the earliest point at which both components come together in the form of full written registration is at the end of the Massoretic activity.

B. *The New Testament.*

1. *General.*

When we turn to the New Testament, the general structure of the problems is very different. The mode of transmission of the text could scarcely be more unlike that of the Hebrew Bible. The peculiar constitution of the Hebrew writing system here does not apply. Unlike the Hebrew Bible situation, the New Testament survived to us in a wide variety of manuscript traditions with a large number of variations which are substantial in point of meaning; thus there are great differences, but problems of basic linguistic intelligibility are low: it is a question which reading is correct, but at least a choice of intelligible readings is available. Again, while the language of the Hebrew Bible could not be paralleled by any substantial body of contemporary Hebrew outside the biblical text, the language of the New Testament can be set against a very large corpus of other contemporary Greek literature, Jewish-Christian and pagan.

2. *Original and translation in the New Testament.*

The only point concerning the New Testament which may deserve comment, in continuity with our discussion of the Hebrew Bible, is the place of a Semitic-language text as the original from which the Greek text descended. The early New Testament story took place in Palestine, in an environment which was at least partly Semitic-speaking, although the importance of Greek in Palestine should not be minimized. The Gospels actually cite some Semitic phrases of Jesus, and a few other Semitic terms appear throughout the New Testament. It has been customary to hold that Jesus's vernacular was Aramaic; but some recent studies have supported the case for Hebrew as well as Aramaic, and some use of Greek by him cannot be ruled out. The New Testament material can therefore be usefully classified as follows:

a. Passages which were originally spoken or written in a Semitic language; e.g., much or most of the teaching of Jesus.

b. Passages which may have been composed in Greek but in a style more or less deliberately imitative of the Greek Old Testament (Septuagint); e.g., perhaps poems like the Magnificat in Luke.

c. Passages (the majority) which were composed in Greek from the beginning.

In this there are several points of interest for any evaluation of the New Testament text as linguistic evidence. First of all, clearly, where a Semitic original is probable, the Greek evidence has to be assessed with this probability in mind. Second, it is possible that misunderstandings have occurred in the passage from Semitic to Greek, and that difficulties in the Greek can be cleared up by a hypothetical retracing of this process.[8] Third, it may at least be theoretically possible, by retracing the process in this way, to reach a more certain decision whether the original language, if Semitic, was Aramaic or Hebrew.

On the other hand, it must be doubted whether the place of this Semitic original can ever be more than 'background' to the Greek New Testament; in other words, in spite of the certainty that conversations reported in the New Testament took place in a Semitic language, there is little real doubt that the Greek text is in every normal sense the 'original' text. The characteristics of 'translation Greek,' as clearly found in the Septuagint and other Greek translations of the Old Testament, are absent in the New Testament or much more thinly spread. In the case of the Old Testament we have a linguistic process of translating a text that was already complete and authoritative. In the New Testament the transfer of material from the Semitic language environment to the Greek may well have taken a different course. Suppose one gives

---

[8]The major modern work is M. Black, *An Aramaic Approach to the Gospels and Acts* (3rd ed., Oxford, 1967).

a lecture in English, and its purport has to be made known to German speakers. One can take the text of the lecture and translate it as a whole into German. But one can also ask a person who was there and heard the lecture, and who also knows both languages, to relate the purport of the lecture to his friends in German and in his own words. It is this latter model that seems more appropriate for the New Testament: in other words, the process of linguistic translation was an incidental part of a process of free religious communication. The formation of a *text* took place in Greek, and in that sense the Greek text can be taken rightly as the original text of the New Testament, with perhaps exceptions for some limited parts.

RECORDS, WRITING, AND DECIPHERMENT

I. J. Gelb

RECORDS, WRITING, AND DECIPHERMENT

I. J. Gelb

1. *Written sources.*

Under written remains, sources, or records we understand texts, inscriptions, manuscripts, books, etc., which represent the written output of an individual, a nation, or any larger human configuration. Knowledge about these written records either has been passed on traditionally from generation to generation or it has been obtained through field explorations and excavations in modern times. Similarly, the understanding of these records either has been preserved through the ages, as in the case of Hebrew or Chinese; or it has been, or will have to be, recovered through decipherment in our times, as in the case of Egyptian hieroglyphic or Mesopotamian cuneiform. Under the general term 'decipherment' we include the recovery of the writing systems and languages, the use of which was brought to a stop, and consequently lost, between the time of their use in the past and their recovery in the present. Written records together with material remains derived from excavations, such as buildings and tools, form the two main bases for our understanding of past civilizations. Evaluation of the written records also leads to the reconstruction of their underlying systems of writing.

It is very difficult, if not impossible, to distinguish the concept of 'written records' from that of 'literature.' Authors of works on literatures of ancient peoples often include under literature the whole body of written remains, as distinguished from material remains such as buildings, tools, weapons, dress, etc. 'Literature' to us means mainly belles-lettres, that is, works created under some kind of artistic, inspirational, or imaginative impulse. What may be called literature in one period or area may not be literature in another. For that reason, I am avoiding the term 'literature' altogether in the following discussion.

The use of writing in written records can be either primary or secondary. Its primary use is found in records whose sole purpose is to convey the written message. Its secondary use is found in records which have another purpose in addition to that of communication, as on inscribed sculptures, reliefs, vases, gems, seals, coins, or measures. The frequency and variety of records available from different areas and periods depend on many factors, the most important of which are the availability and cost of writing materials, their perishability, and the widely varying degrees of application of writing.

The recovery of written records of dead civilizations is tied up with the progress of field explorations and excavations. Before systematic archeological activities began early in the nineteenth century in Asia and Africa, our knowledge of ancient Near Eastern civilizations was limited to what could be gathered from the Bible and Classical sources. This was very little indeed, certainly for the great civilizations which surrounded Palestine, if not for Palestine proper. It can be said without any exaggeration that almost our entire knowledge of ancient civilizations such as Egypt and Mesopotamia is derived from the efforts of the explorers and excavators in the field. Certain areas of the ancient Near East have been explored more thoroughly than others. Mesopotamia and Egypt are well explored, but hundreds of sites still remain to be excavated. Relatively little known are eastern Anatolia, Syria, and Iran. No Median sites have as yet been discovered, and as a result our knowledge about the Medes does not go much beyond what we have known for years from Greek sources. The best explored and excavated area in the Near East is Biblical Palestine; contrary to expectations, however, attestation of written records from Palestine is very meager.

Progress in discoveries in the ancient Near East often follows the proverbial 'excavator's luck.' It was at two Assyrian sites, Nineveh and Dur-Sharrukin, that the excavators discovered the great archives which paved the way for our understanding of the Mesopotamian languages, and not at Babylon, which yielded great palaces but scanty written attestation. And it was Knossos and Pylos—not Troy and Mycenae—that provided us with written records which formed the basis for the recovery of the older languages of the Aegean area. For years Ras Shamra was one of the hundreds of sites in Syria unknown to and untouched by archaeology. In 1928, a chance discovery of a stone inscription at the site by a native plowman led to important excavations in subsequent years which have unfolded for us the most varied collection of written records ever made in the ancient Near East: Ugaritic, Amorite, Akkadian, Sumerian, Hurrian, Hittite, Egyptian, and Aegean.

The extent to which the frequency and variety of written records is connected with the degree of literacy in a given area cannot be discussed due to lack of data. My feeling is that the connections are negligible. Another point which cannot be profitably discussed here because of lack of data is the relation of written to oral tradition. It is quite plausible that certain genres, such as epics, legends, historical narratives, popular songs, and proverbs, have traditionally been preserved from generation to generation by word of mouth rather than in writing. In some areas and periods, a taboo against the use of writing for certain literary or magical genres may explain their lack of attestation.

I know of no systematic treatment of written records, their form, material, function, etc. For preliminary thoughts on the topic, cf. Gelb 1973.

2. *Epigraphy and paleography.*

The investigation of writing from the textual point of view has been traditionally the prime domain of the epigrapher and paleographer. While epigraphy is concerned mainly with inscriptions written in characters incised or scratched with a sharp tool on hard material, such as stone or metal, paleography deals mainly with manuscripts written in characters drawn or painted with pen, pencil, or brush on soft material, such as leather, papyrus, or paper. Since epigraphy means 'writing on something' and paleography means 'old writing,' it is clear that the distinction made above between epigraphy and paleography cannot be justified on etymological grounds. This distinction has grown artificially over the years, as one scholar or another began to apply one or the other term to his own branch of study of written sources. Owing to the close interrelations between epigraphy and paleography, some scholars refuse to admit any distinction between the two, and prefer to use one of the two terms for both disciplines.

The main characteristics of epigraphy and paleography as listed above may be applied, with some leeway, to the ancient Near East (Mesopotamia, Egypt, Anatolia, etc.), the Classical world, China, India, the Islamic world, and, in general, to Western writings from the Middle Ages on. But there are many difficulties and exceptions.

Paleography and epigraphy are involved in the study of written sources from two points of view: the purely formal aspect and the hermeneutical aspect.

The study of the purely formal aspect, possible without any understanding of the contents or without an extended study of the contents, is concerned, for example, with the kind, form, and size of the materials used, with the technique of writing, and with the form, order, and direction of writing. Hermeneutics, possible only with study of the contents, is concerned with the dating and localizing of written sources, their authorship, linguistic interpretation, content evaluation, and the like.

A general scientific discipline of epigraphy and paleography does not exist. There are no studies which treat of the subject from a general, theoretical point of view, encompassing all the written sources, wherever they may be found. The narrow fields which are represented are, e.g., West Semitic epigraphy, Arabic paleography, Greek and/or Latin epigraphy and/or paleography, or Chinese epigraphy and/or paleography. In all cases these narrow fields of study form subdivisions of wider, but still linguistically or geographically defined areas of study, such as Semitic or Arabic philology, Classical philology, Assyriology, Sinology, etc. Cf. also Gelb 1974 and Puhvel 1975.

3. *Language and writing.*

Very little work has been done in the field of relations of writing to language. Philologists have been concerned mainly with the historical evolution of writing and have paid little attention to the interrelations between writing and language. Linguists have been more concerned with the spoken language than with the written language. When interested in written languages, they have often limited their study to living written languages, neglecting the rich sources of information which can be culled from ancient written languages, especially those written in pre-alphabetic systems. The relation of writing to language has been pursued in recent years mainly by scholars with a background in linguistics. Because of their interest in modern languages and writings, this generally implies relations between the alphabet and language. Due to the preference for a synchronic-descriptive approach rather than diachronic-historical, linguists generally have stressed the independent character of writing and have studied it as an independent system, rather than as a system ultimately based on and related to the underlying language. Both approaches seem justified to me. Scholars have as much right to point out the close interrelations between writing and language as they have to study writing as a relatively closed system, without being involved in matters of relationships between writing and language and the degree of their interdependence.

While the connections between language and writing are very close, there has never been a one-to-one correspondence between the elements of language and the signs of writing. The 'fit' (a term used by Gleason 1955, p. 302; Voegelin and Voegelin 1961, pp. 85 f.) between language and writing is generally stronger in the earlier stages of a certain system of writing and weaker in its later stages. This is due to the fact that a writing system when first introduced generally reproduces rather faithfully the underlying phonemic structure. In the course of time writing, more conservative than language, generally does not keep up with the continuous changes in a language and, as time progresses, diverges more and more from its linguistic counterpart. A good example is the old Latin writing system, with its relatively good 'fit' between graphemes and phonemes, as compared with present-day French or English writing with their tremendous divergencies between graphemes and phonemes. In some cases, recent spelling reforms have helped to remedy the existing discrepancies between writing and language. The best 'fit' between phonemes and graphemes has been achieved in Korean writing in the sixteenth century and in the Finnish and Czech systems of modern times.

Families of writing systems are not related to families of languages. Note, for example, that English and Finnish are written in the Latin system but belong to two different families of languages, and that cuneiform writing was used in antiquity by peoples speaking many different languages.

The temporal primacy of language over writing has been taken for granted by most scholars, especially American linguists. It has been contested by some European scholars who claim that writing is as old as oral language and gesture language. The fact is that full writing, expressing linguistic elements, originated only about five thousand years ago in Mesopotamia and Egypt and full writing is therefore much younger than language. Only if we include the semasiographic stage under writing can the assumption of equal temporal hierarchy of writing and language be admitted. As noted elsewhere, however, the semasiographic stage should not be treated as full writing, but as a forerunner of writing. Cf. Gelb 1974.

4. *Philology and linguistics.*

There is a good deal of confusion regarding the aims and methods of the fields of philology and linguistics. Philology, involved mainly in the study of the linguistic sources of a people or a group of peoples, forms the basic means for the comprehension of their respective cultures. It deals less with oral sources than with written sources, mainly literature (whatever its exact meaning). Philology deals with the formal aspects of writing under the topic of epigraphy and paleography. Linguistics is concerned with the study of linguistic systems as reconstructed mainly from oral sources. Pursued less than the study of 'oral language,' the study of the 'written language,' that is, of the language as it is used in written sources, is also a matter of linguistics. Linguistics deals with the structural aspects of writing under the heading of 'graphemics.' Cf. Gelb 1974.

5. *Semiotics.*

Men communicate with each other by means of various systems of signs, of which the most universal are oral language or speech, a system of auditory communication, and gesture language and writing, two systems of visual communication. For the general science of signs several terms have been proposed, of which the term 'semiotic' (used by Morris 1946, p. 3 f.) or 'semiotics' (as here preferred) is the most appropriate. The term 'semantics,' which deals with the meaning of linguistic elements, should be carefully distinguished from the much broader term 'semiotics.' For these and other terms, see Read 1948, pp. 78-97, Sebeok et al. 1964, pp. 5f. and 275 f., and Gelb 1974.

6. *Grammatology.*

The field of study which deals with writing in the broadest sense was called 'grammatology' by Gelb 1952, p. 23 (= Gelb 1958, p. 31), following partially the term 'grammatography,' which was used in 1861 in a title of a book on writing by Ballhorn published in England. The original German edition, from which the English translation was made, does not use the term. Equally appropriate as 'grammatology' are the terms 'grammatonomy' used by Boodberg 1957, p. 113, and 'graphonomy' used by Hockett 1958, p. 539. Not acceptable are 'graphology' of Halliday 1961, p. 244, because this term already has another, well-established meaning; and 'graphemics,' because this term is too narrow. Cf. also Gelb 1968 and Gelb 1974.

7. *Graphemics.*

The field of graphemics deals with full writing or phonography, as represented in systems of writing in which written signs generally have set correspondences with elements of language. Graphemics is concerned mainly with the graphemes of a system, that is, such signs as phonemograms, syllabograms, and morphograms, which find their equivalents in phonemes, syllables, and morphemes of a language. Thus the field of graphemics deals with writing after it became a secondary transfer of the language, a vehicle by which elements of the spoken language were expressed in a more or less exact form by means of visual signs used conventionally. This took place for the first time about five thousand years ago in the Sumerian and Egyptian graphic systems.

Instead of 'graphemics,' other scholars use the terms 'graphics' (Francis 1958) or 'graphic linguistics' (Crossland 1956). All three terms are frequently misused by scholars who limit the terms to the study of alphabetic writings, overlooking or paying scant attention to all other types of writing, such as the logo-syllabic and syllabic systems. Cf. also Gelb 1968 and Gelb 1974.

8. *Auxiliary disciplines.*

There are a number of scholarly disciplines which have some relation to the study of writing. The most important among them are: art, religion, cultural anthropology, child psychology, human pathology (amnesic aphasia), and animal ethology (biosemiotics). Cf. the extensive treatment in Gelb 1974.

9. *Types of writing systems.*

A chart showing the typology of writing is given below to enable readers to understand the terminology and classification of writing as used in the section devoted to methods of decipherment.

Scholars interested in descriptive and historical presentations of the various systems of writing should consult Gelb 1963, Jensen 1969, Diringer 1968, Février 1959, Cohen 1958, Istrin 1965, Friedrich 1966b or Barthel 1972.

NO WRITING: Pictures

FORERUNNERS OF WRITING: Semasiography
  1. Descriptive-Representational Devices
  2. Identifying-Mnemonic Devices

FULL WRITING: Phonography

1. *Logo-Syllabic:*	Sumerian + Akkadian + Hittite cuneiform	Egyptian	Proto-Elamite	Proto-Indic	Cretan	Hittite hiero-glyphs	Chinese + Chinese-derived systems
2. *Syllabic:*	*Type A* (with vowel indication)	*Type B* (without vowel indication)			*Type A* (with vowel indication)		*Type A* (with vowel indication)
	Cuneiform Syllabaries:	*West Semitic Syllabaries:*			*Aegean Syllabaries:*		Japanese Syllabary
	Elamite Hurrian Urartian Hattic Luwian Palaic, etc.	Proto-Sinaitic Proto-Palestinian Phoenician Hebrew Aramaic, etc.			Linear A Linear B Phaistos disk Proto-Byblian Cypro-Minoan Cypriote		
	Mixed Syllabic B + A	Ugaritic Persian Cuneiform					
	Mixed Syllabic A + Alphabetic	Iberian					
3. *Alphabetic:*		Greek Aramaic (vocalized) Hebrew (vocalized) Latin Indic Korean, etc.					

10. *Grammatology and decipherment.*

A basic prerequisite to a successful decipherment consists of a thorough acquaintance with the field of grammatology, specifically the structure and typology of writing. This should enable scholars to answer primary questions as to whether the texts to be deciphered represent real writing or no writing, original writing or forgeries, and should be helpful in indicating to scholars the type to which the particular writing belongs, i.e., alphabetic, syllabic, or word-syllabic. It may sound rather preposterous to ask a scholar to take a stand on the question of whether the texts he is studying do or do not represent writing, but even such well-known systems as the cuneiform and the hieroglyphic Egyptian were for a time considered by some scholars as merely ornamental or symbolic, and it was not until the nineteenth century that scholars were able to provide evidence that the two systems represent real writing systems.

There are written remains, especially those appearing in bilingual versions, that have so many of the obvious characteristics of writing that scholars may be forgiven if they fail to provide evidence that the texts in question represent writing; but this is not always the case, and all too often scholars have failed to provide such evidence when it was required. I have in mind primarily the question of the Rongo-rongo boards of Easter Island which are generally taken to be composed in a real writing system, but which I have characterized as nothing else than a series of pictorial representations concocted for magical purposes.

The question as to whether certain written remains are original or modern forgeries can often be answered with the help of grammatology. Modern forgeries are spurious fabrications usually made by or for dealers in antiquities for the purpose of financial profit; some well-known fakes were made for the purpose of national glorification, while other hoaxes were perpetrated by scholars for amusement, I assume. Among the best-known forgeries of modern times are the 'Glozel finds' in France, whose authenticity was defended tenaciously by the renowned French archeologist S. Reinach. On the other hand, the Phaistos Disk in Crete and the Stone of King Mesha of Moab, once thought spurious by many scholars, are now almost universally considered to be authentic.

Knowledge of grammatology appears to be most useful to scholars in the definition of the type of writing on which they are working. From a practical point of view, this is also the most common application of grammatology to the field of decipherment. It is relatively easy to count the number of graphemes, i.e., of signs with distinctive features, in a given writing system. The number might total about sixty graphemes. The teachings of grammatology tell us that a writing consisting of about sixty graphemes should represent a syllabary. Similarly, if the number of the counted graphemes reaches several hundred, it is safe to assume in the light of grammatology that the underlying writing represents a logo-syllabic system.

11. *Methods of decipherment.*

In contrast to the extensive literature in the field of cryptology, both scholarly and popular, there is a lamentable dearth on the subject of the decipherment of extinct writings and languages. More often than not, the decipherers themselves have failed to preface their work with any remarks on their methodology. The history of decipherment is treated in Friedrich 1966a, a book which has also appeared in English and Russian versions. The latter contains extensive additions by I. M. Diakonoff.

More or less popular accounts of decipherment can be found in Doblhofer 1957, Cleator 1959, Gordon 1968, Cottrell 1971, Barber and Pope 1975. A bulky volume on cryptanalysis, written by an ex-journalist, David Kahn 1967, has a chapter on extinct writings and languages, uneven in quality. Good discussions of the decipherment of individual writings are to be found in standard manuals on writing by Jensen (1969), Diringer (1968), Février (1959), Cohen (1958), Istrin (1965), and Friedrich (1966).

I know of only two relatively brief studies dedicated to the methodology of decipherment as such, Modrze 1930 and Aalto 1954. One can also consult the section "Methodisches zur Entschliessung verschollener Schriften und Sprachen" in Friedrich (1966a, pp. 123-8). Some thoughts on the cultural basis of decipherment are expressed in Voegelin and Voegelin 1963. My own thoughts on the methodology of decipherment were offered in Gelb 1973. [Reworked completely with the assistance of

Robert M. Whiting, the section on decipherment was presented at the three-day International Symposium on Undeciphered Languages organized in celebration of the 150th anniversary of the Royal Asiatic Society in London during the summer of 1973.]

There are many stories connected with the decipherment of ancient writings and the recovery of forgotten languages, but they need not be retold here. Furthermore, these accounts usually deal only with the discovery of the key, that brief moment of insight when some datum is arrived at, which when inserted causes the rest of the puzzle to fall into place. But what we are interested in here is the tremendous amount of work, routine but necessary, which precedes that moment and makes it possible, and the even larger task and labor which follow that moment and result in the recovery of the language.

There is a clear connection between the decipherment of extinct writings and languages used for the purpose of normal communication, and cryptanalysis, which deals with the decipherment of writings used for the purpose of secret communication. For this reason, it is frequently convenient to use the terminology of cryptology when referring to the problems encountered by the decipherer of ancient writing systems. However, one important difference should be stressed. Cryptography or secret writing attempts to lay obstacles in the path of the non-intended reader which will hopefully make the interpretation of the message impossible, while the writing systems used by the ancients were meant for direct communication with the reader. This is important because of the linguistic feature of 'redundancy' which the designers of cryptographic systems try to eliminate to the greatest extent possible.

In spoken language, redundancy allows us to understand what has been said even if some of the sounds are not heard or are badly distorted, because of the fact that certain sequences of sounds are more frequent than others while some sequences do not occur at all. Thus if several phonemes of an utterance are missed, our knowledge of the sound patterns of the language allows us to eliminate very quickly the sound sequences which are not allowed and to reconstruct the one which is. If more than one sequence is allowable, context usually permits us to make the final decision. This same feature of redundancy is also present in writing systems: certain combinations of signs are more frequent than others while some do not occur at all. Most of the methods of decipherment make use of this fact, and the degree of difficulty or ease with which a writing system can be deciphered depends in large measure on the extent to which this feature can be recognized and exploited.

Full systems of writing express language on two levels, morphological (logography) or phonetic (syllabary, alphabet). This gives rise to three basic types of full writing systems: logo-syllabic, syllabic, and alphabetic. The latter two types are phonetic while the first combines morphological elements (logograms) and phonetic elements (syllabograms). Even so, the syllabic and alphabetic systems usually contain morphemic elements to a greater or lesser degree. In cryptography, replacement of phonetic elements is called 'cipher,' while replacement of morphemes is known as 'code.' There are two basic types of cipher, substitution and transposition.

Redundancy is also present at the morphemic level, but since the number of morphemes in a language is so much greater than the number of phonemes, the effect of redundant morphemes is not as great as that of phonetic redundancy. For this reason, a code is generally harder to break than a cipher; and a writing system based mainly on logograms will be more difficult to decipher than one based on phonograms, given the same degree of availability of materials and of knowledge of the underlying language.

The preceding statement implies that the degree to which the underlying language of a writing system is known affects the decipherment of the writing system. This can be stated more strongly: Provided sufficient text is available, a phonetic system of writing can and ultimately must be deciphered if the underlying language is known. It should be noted, however, that the converse is not true. Interpretation of a language is a matter of linguistic analysis which determines the morphological and syntactic rules governing it. These rules are much more extensive and complicated than the phonological ones and hence it is much more difficult to deduce the former from the latter than vice versa. In view of this, we should really speak of 'decipherment' in connection with writing systems and of the 'recovery' or 'interpretation' of languages. In popular usage, however, the term decipherment is also used in connection with languages, as when one speaks of 'the decipherment of Etruscan.'

Using the term decipherment in its wider sense, we can classify decipherments into several types based on the extent of our knowledge of the two elements involved, the writing system and the language. There are four possible situations, only three of which present problems to the decipherer.

The four categories are:

Type 0:   known writing and known language
Type I: unknown writing and known language
Type II: known writing and unknown language
Type III: unknown writing and unknown language

It must be pointed out here that 'known' and 'unknown' in this application are not absolutes but shade into each other in a manner which cannot be expressed quantitatively. This is especially true of languages, where we can speak of a well-known one such as Latin, or a less-known one such as Sumerian or Hurrian, or a virtually unknown one such as Etruscan. Furthermore, a language may be unknown itself but be more or less closely related to a known language or group of languages, a fact which, once established, moves it closer to the category of a known language.

Keeping this in mind, we shall return to our four types of decipherments. Type 0 (zero), a known language written in a known writing system, is generally considered trivial and requires little discussion. However, despite the fact that this type offers no difficulty in decipherment, examples of it can provide us with valuable information, especially if the writing system is other than the one normally used for the language. I am thinking here of the inscriptions written in the Phoenician (Punic) language but using the Greek or Latin alphabet, thus furnishing useful information for the vocalization of that language that is not expressed by its normal writing system; and of the limited amount of Sumerian and Akkadian material written in the Greek alphabet, which not only increases our phonological knowledge of these languages, but also serves as a convenient check on the validity of the decipherment of cuneiform.

Type 0 corresponds to what is known in cryptography as 'plaintext,' that is, an uncoded message.

Decipherments of Type I, an unknown writing system used for a known language, vary in degree of difficulty depending on the nature of the writing system. We have already seen that there are three basic types of writing systems: alphabetic, syllabic, and logo-syllabic. Deciphering these writings makes extensive use of the techniques of cryptanalysis.

If the writing system is alphabetic, the problem resembles that of a simple substitution cipher and, provided sufficient text is available, is very easy to solve utilizing the redundancy features of the known language.

If the writing is syllabic, the problem is slightly more complex because of the larger number of graphemes and their more complex phonetic structure. However, syllabaries have their own redundancy features and such a system will eventually succumb to analysis. It should be noted that the amount of text required to guarantee a unique solution of such a system is considerably larger than for an alphabetic system. It is for this reason that the Phaistos syllabary, which probably hides a known language, remains undeciphered. There is just not enough text available to provide an unambiguous solution.

If the writing system is logo-syllabic, the problem can become quite complex. It amounts to code mixed with polygraphic encipherment. It has already been noted that code is considerably harder to break than cipher. For this reason the proper cryptanalytical procedure would be to attack the cipher (syllabograms) first and then deduce the code (logograms) from the knowledge of the morpholexical structure of the language. On the practical level, other factors often intervene which simplify this process, as we shall see when we discuss methodology.

The history of Type I decipherments bears out this general picture. Thus of the writings in this category, the most easily deciphered have been the Phoenician and Ugaritic writings, which consist of only 22 to 30 signs. (Although syllabic in nature, from the point of view of cryptology these systems behave like alphabets.) More difficult problems were posed by the Old Persian, Cypriote, and Linear B systems—all of the class of syllabaries— with the number of signs varying from approximately 40 to 80. Much more difficult were the decipherment of logo-syllabic systems such as Egyptian hieroglyphic, Akkadian cuneiform, and Hittite hieroglyphic, involving hundreds of signs.

Type II decipherments are not, as we have already noted, strictly speaking, decipherments, but rather linguistic analysis. The category of an unknown language corresponds in cryptography to code, which involves the substitution of an unknown linguistic element for a known one. Such systems are extremely difficult to break, and a language which is truly unknown is virtually impossible to reconstruct using cryptanalytic methods because of the tremendous amount of text required. This is not to deny the possibility of reconstructing an unknown language, but only to indicate the very low probability of recovering a significant part of it by internal means alone. In every case of a Type II decipherment, external sources of information have played a large role. Even if a language cannot easily be recovered by internal means, it is still possible to construct a formal (descriptive) grammar of such a language by making a catalog of short repetitive elements and classifying them as affixes or function words (as opposed to content words), even though their meaning or use may be unknown. This describes our present state of knowledge about the Etruscan language, for example.

Type III decipherments, involving an unknown writing system and an unknown language, are clearly the most difficult of all. If such a case occurs in cultural isolation where no outside information can be brought to bear, it can be considered undecipherable. External sources can sometimes provide clues which can reduce it to a Type I or Type II problem. If the language is truly unknown, reduction to Type II is not a significant improvement in understandability. As we have seen, our knowledge of the phonetic shape of Etruscan does little to reduce its obscurity.

Type III situations have been compared by some authors to the cryptographic category of enciphered code, but this is not true. Cryptographic codes have no phonological shape since the code words are usually series of unrelated symbols. An unknown language is code whether it can be read or not. The purpose of enciphering code is to further reduce redundancy by making frequently used code words appear differently at different places in the text. In Type III, these repetitive morphemes are clearly visible and can be collected to form a preliminary grammar of the language in exactly the same manner as described for Type II.

Having outlined the types of decipherment which may be encountered and having assessed their relative difficulty, let us consider some of the methods involved in decipherment.

Past approaches to the recovery of extinct and unknown writings and languages have been almost uniformly characterized by haphazard touch-and-go procedures. With very few laudable exceptions, the would-be decipherers have approached their task without any idea of cryptanalytic techniques. In the light of this almost total lack of systematic methodology, it is astonishing to note how frequently the tenacious efforts of scholars have led to a successful decipherment.

From a cryptanalytic point of view, we can distinguish two broad areas of methodology. These deal with the utilization of *external information,* or what can be determined about the probable contents of the cryptogram from outside sources, and *internal information,* or what can be learned from an analysis of the cryptogram itself. Every cryptogram has a certain *a priori* probability of containing a given message. If the cryptanalyst can guess what the message is, the solution of the cryptogram will be much easier. Even having only a general idea about what the message might be will facilitate decipherment.

In considering the application of this concept to ancient writings, it is interesting to note that frequently the key to a decipherment has been provided by a source external to the writing under study. In most cases, this has been one or more proper names known traditionally, such as the Persian royal names found in Herodotus, or provided by a bilingual inscription, such as the Rosetta Stone, to name just two of the best known examples.

Therefore, efore doing any work on the decipherment of a specific writing or language, a would-be decipherer must become acquainted with the historical-geographical background of the area from which it comes. One should remember the case of Champollion, who spent years familiarizing himself with the history, geography, religion, and languages of Egypt as preserved in the Classical sources or by tradition, before he dared even to suggest the reading of a single sign of the Egyptian writing system.

It is generally considered that a bilingual text is a type of external information which will immediately produce a unique solution of an ancient writing or language. The reasons why this is not true will become apparent if we remember the cryptological analogies which we have established. If a cryptanalyst has both the plain and enciphered text of a message, his problem is solved since ciphering is a linear and reversible transformation of one writing system into another. Furthermore, this information allows him to determine the key, that is, the rules under which the transformation was made. But we have already established that the only class of decipherment which corresponds to cryptographic cipher is Type I, a known language written in an unknown writing, and that this corresponds to simple substitution cipher. It can easily be shown that for substitution cipher, the choice of the cipher alphabet does not affect the general appearance of the cipher text; or in other words, all substitution encipherments of a given message are equivalent and all that is significant is the pattern of letter repetition. But the patterns of letter repetition are generated by the language, or, more specifically, by the redundancy features of the language. The immediate conclusion is that, provided there is sufficient text for these redundancy features to assert themselves, the only key necessary for the solution of a substitution cryptogram is the language in which it is written!

The reason that having a bilingual text is not equivalent to a cryptanalyst having the plain and enciphered text of a message is the simple fact that the two parts of the bilingual ARE NOT WRITTEN IN THE SAME LANGUAGE. Hence we are not dealing with an enciphered version of the same text, but rather with an encoded version of it. While encipherment is a linear reversible process, translation is not, as anyone who has given any thought to the problem of machine translation quickly realizes. Translation of a passage of moderate length into another language and then back into the original by another translator would almost never result in exactly the same text as the original. If a cryptanalyst has the plaintext and encoded version of a message, he cannot guarantee a unique solution for each code group; and even if by chance he could, knowledge of a hundred or so code groups would hardly make a dent in a code consisting of ten thousand groups.

Of what value, then, are bilingual texts to the decipherer of ancient writings and languages? Let us consider this in the light of the possible types of decipherment. Since the known language of the bilingual represents a coded version of the unknown one, for

Type II and III decipherments which represent code, this means that we now have the same text encoded in two different systems, one of which is known. This allows us to determine some, if not all, of the unknown code groups. As we have seen, unless this number is quite large no significant increase in our knowledge is gained. Thus for Type II decipherments our understanding of Sumerian has been advanced quite far by the tremendous amount of Akkadian-Sumerian bilingual material available, while the relatively short Etruscan-Punic bilingual recently discovered at Pyrgi in Italy has added little to our knowledge of Etruscan.

For Type III decipherments the situation is similar. But there is an important extra. Apparent Type III situations frequently hide a less difficult decipherment, usually Type I, and a bilingual sometimes allows us to break a code group which makes this apparent. This is exactly what happened during the decipherment of the Cypriote syllabary using a Cypriote-Phoenician bilingual. The language turned out to be Greek, but because the redundancy features were altered by the writing conventions of the syllabic script from those expected of classical Greek, it was unrecognizable as such when deciphered.

Another feature of bilingual inscriptions which requires discussion brings us back to our original reason for rejecting the bilingual as an immediate solution, namely that it represents code, not cipher. Cryptographic codes always have groups for a syllabary as well as an alphabet so that words not included in the code can be spelled out. The most frequent need for these groups is to express proper names. Proper names are usually not translated into another language, but are simply transcribed. Thus if a bilingual text has a proper name in one version and the exact position of this name can be located in the other, one can consider the two occurrences as one phonological sequence expressed in two writing systems, or cipher. Since the plaintext is known, the phonetic values of the signs used to encipher it may be established. If enough such occurrences could be found, a Type III situation could be reduced to Type II, and if during the process enough information about the language were found to indicate that the language was known, it would quickly reduce to Type 0.

Finally, a bilingual can be useful as a check on a decipherment made by other means. It should be noted here, however, that not all bilingual inscriptions are well suited to this use, since

the two sections might be either very reliable, verbatim translations, or one might be simply a loose paraphrase of the other.

Although other sources of external information may come to
bear on the decipherment, it is best to shift at this point to internal
analysis and see what preliminary steps should be taken.

Equally as important as a thorough study of the area from
which the writing to be deciphered comes is a sound acquaintance
with the field of grammatology, specifically the structure and
typology of writing. See above, Section 10.

From a consideration of the writing system as a whole, we
move to 'graphotactics' or the evaluation of such graphic characteristics as the position, sequence, arrangement, and direction of
signs, and word division. The sequence of signs in a sign group may
be orderly (as in classical Latin writing) or disorderly (as in the
earliest Sumerian writing). The sequence of signs may be from left
to right, from right to left, or both; or from top to bottom, or
from top to bottom in the sequence of individual signs but from
right to left in the sequence of columns or rows of signs. Word
division may not be indicated at all in the writing, or it may be indicated by special marks in the form of dots or strokes, or by a
space.

More information about the probable content of the inscription can be deduced from repetitive schematic arrangements within the text. Such a repetitive sequence is called a 'routine.'
Routines offer exceedingly valuable information of a quasi-
bilingual nature and are usually easy to detect without any elaborate statistical analysis. For example, if the last line of a text
includes a fairly low numeral, it is a reasonable assumption that it
is a date routine, and one should expect the word 'year' and perhaps a royal name. Similarly if there are numbers throughout the
text and the last line includes a higher number with a word before
it, it is almost certain that the word is 'total.'

Still another source of information about the probable content of an inscription can be utilized if the script is logo-syllabic.
This source is the interpretation of logograms. It was pointed out
earlier that an unknown logo-syllabic system could be considered
to be a mixture of enciphered text and code. While the comparison
is typologically valid, no cryptographer would ever use such a

system. Because even a small amount of context can be extremely valuable in solving a cryptogram, there is absolute prohibition in cryptography against plaintext appearing in the body of an encrypted message. For the same reason, no cryptographer would risk having code groups recognized among the enciphered text, and would insert the code groups at the plaintext level and then encipher both. But ancient writing systems did not strive for secrecy and the logograms are in full view of the decipherer.

If a logo-syllabic writing appears in a Type II situation (known writing, unknown language), the interpretation of all logograms may be known, a situation which generates numerous context clues. The key to Cuneiform Hittite was actually discovered in this manner. If a logo-syllabic system is unknown but largely pictographic, it may be possible to deduce the interpretation of some logograms from their pictorial representations. This is more often true of logograms denoting nouns than of those denoting verbs. But there are pitfalls in this approach because in a logo-syllabic system, syllabograms have usually developed from logograms by means of phonetic transfer, and one must be certain that he is not trying to interpret a syllabic sign as a logogram.

There are several other ways of distinguishing and interpreting logograms. Logograms are at times distinguished from syllabograms by a special mark. In a sign group composed of several signs, it is frequently possible to assume that the first or sometimes the first two signs represent the logogram, and the rest of the signs denote the syllabic indicators. Finally, semantic indicators or determinatives preceding or following a logogram help in distinguishing logograms and at the same time, because they are logograms themselves, help in ascertaining the sphere of meaning to which they belong.

The limitations involved in the understanding of logograms without being able to read them phonetically form no great obstacle to the understanding of texts. There are well-known and fully developed writing systems, such as Sumerian and Cuneiform Hittite, which abound in logograms with clear meaning but unknown reading. If we can interpret all the logograms of a logo-syllabic system, the residue is obviously a syllabic system with plaintext clues scattered through it. Such a system would a priori be easier to solve than a normal syllabic one.

Having exhausted all sources of information about the probable content of the text, if the system still remains undeciphered, the next step is a systematic application of statistics to determine the redundancy characteristics of the writing or the language. Statistical analysis involves making frequency lists of the individual signs, of sequences of signs, and of signs which appear more frequently in initial or final position in a word than others. These statistics about the frequency with which certain signs appear in combinations or in certain positions in fact attest to the redundancy features of the language which generated them, perhaps modified by the limitations and orthographic conventions of the writing system employed. Thus, for example, an orthography which does not express double consonants will distort the redundancy features of a language that does. This is a problem which has to be resolved by outside information, since the distortion of the redundancy features will make the enciphered language appear to be different, or, more likely, unknown. However, if some phonetic values can be established the language will soon be recognized, even with this reduced redundancy, because redundancy is merely a measure of how much of a transmitted message can be omitted without impairing its intelligibility.

Another useful outcome of statistics, especially for syllabic systems of the Aegean type (only single vowels and consonant-plus-vowel signs), is the possibility of constructing a grid system which limits the phonetic values which may be assigned to a given sign by grouping together the signs which interchange under certain circumstances. By this method it is possible to group together signs which should have the same consonant but a different vowel, or alternatively, the same vowel but a different consonant. These groupings may be arranged to form a grid with the consonant as one coordinate, and the vowel as the other. All this may be accomplished without being able to read a single sign. The usefulness of the grid stems from the fact that once a few phonetic values are determined, the rest fall into place almost automatically.

I think that this discussion of statistics is the proper place to mention the application of computers to decipherment. The compilation of statistical analyses I have described can be a very laborious process, especially if the amount of textual material available is large. In accomplishing this work, computers can be utilized most profitably. I estimate that the use of a computer in my work on Amorite has saved me several man-years of tedious repetitive labor. However, while the computer is very useful for collecting, sorting, and counting, analysis should, at least at present, be left to the human mind. The computer has the same problems with ancient languages as with modern ones, and the same limitations which presently make computer translations unreliable, except for very narrow purposes, hinder their usefulness in analyzing ancient languages.

The first attempt to decipher an ancient writing with the help of computers was the decipherment of Maya writing by Russian scholars. While the results are disappointing, the method is sound and may hold promise for the future. The first step was the collection of both linguistic and graphic data from available sources. Next the redundancy features of both the linguistic and graphic data were determined by computer. Finally, the output of the linguistic and graphic data was correlated in order to reach certain conclusions as to the reading or meaning of the Maya signs on the basis of comparable frequencies and distribution within the Maya linguistic material. It is my belief that the failure of the decipherment is not due primarily to flaws of methodology, but to the fact that Mayan glyphs do not represent a full phonetic writing system. The decipherment is apparently of Type I (unknown writing, known language), and we have already shown that for this category, provided sufficient text is available, a phonetic writing can, and ultimately must, be deciphered if the underlying language is known. Since there is plenty of Mayan text available and the language is known, the fact that the writing has defied even the most sophisticated attempts at decipherment leads me to the conclusion that it is not a phonetic writing system. Therefore the lack of success by the computer does not diminish its potential for this type of decipherment.

I have left the discussion of the assumption of an underlying language until late in my paper because it is involved in the test of a decipherment. But I have tried to stress, both in my discussion of the types of decipherment and elsewhere, that the extent to which the underlying language is known or can be recognized as known determines almost completely the difficulty of the decipherment. Hence the assumption of an underlying language is one of the most basic premises of the decipherment. If the assumption of the underlying language is wrong, then the decipherment is wrong. Note, however, that the decipherment may progress up to a point even if the assumption of the language is wrong. A good example is Linear B, where a grid structure for many of the signs had been worked out, but which remained undeciphered as long as it was assumed that its underlying language was Etruscan.

A preliminary assumption of an underlying language is the result of logical deductions about the linguistic situation in the area from which the writing or the language to be deciphered comes. The assumption is more or less self-evident in the great majority of cases. Thus it was logical to assume that ancient Egyptian would be a language ancestral to Coptic (spoken in Egypt until quite recently), just as it was plausible to start with the presupposition that the language of the Ugaritic texts would be a Semitic one, closely related to the other Semitic languages known from the general area, such as Phoenician, Aramaic, and Hebrew. The probabilities as to the underlying language had to be weighed in varying degrees in the case of other decipherments, such as Hieroglyphic Hittite, Linear B, Cypriote, and Iberian.

The assumption of an underlying language may be plausible or even probable, but no decipherment is possible if the assumed language has no parallels in any known group of languages. This may be the case for Cretan hieroglyphic, which may be the writing system for Minoan, a native Mediterranean language possibly unrelated to any other known language.

As a test of decipherment, we should insist on the translation of a full text, not simply excerpts. It is frequently possible to provide a persuasive interpretation for a small portion of the text, such as a phrase or even a sentence, but this cannot be a decipherment if the rest of the text is gibberish. The translation of the text must be consonant with the preliminary expectations about the contents of the text. It is reasonable to assume that Proto-Elamite texts, full of numbers and measures, would represent simple administrative accounts dealing with the day-by-day routine of running a household, such as the listing of incoming and outgoing commodities. A decipherment that would read magic conjurations into these texts would be highly suspect.

Undoubtedly the best test of a decipherment is repeatability. That is, it should be possible to decipher another text, preferably one the original decipherer has not seen, using the decipherer's

methods. Perhaps the most spectacular example of this was con-
clusive proof of the correctness of the decipherment of Linear B
provided by the discovery of the famous 'tripod' text, which not
only deciphered into good Greek words, but also had pictographic
representations which showed exactly the objects which those
words represented.

Note: The present article is a slightly revised version of the
article printed in *Visible Language* VIII (1974), pp. 293-318,
which in turn is an adaptation from the paper read at the Ann
Arbor symposium.

12. *Bibliography.*

AALTO, PENNTI. 1945. "Notes on methods of decipherment of
unknown writings and languages." *Studia Orientalia* 11/4.

BALLHORN, FRIEDRICH. 1861. *A manual of reference to the
alphabets of ancient and modern languages.* London, 1861.
Translated from German.

BARBER, E. J. W. 1975. *Archaeological Decipherment.* Princeton,
N.J. (Announced but not yet available.)

BARTHEL, GUSTAV. 1972. "Konnte Adam schreiben?" Welt-
geschichte der Schrift. Köln.

BOODBERG, PETER. 1957. "The Chinese script: An essay on
nomenclature (the First Hecaton)." Studies presented to
Yuen Ren Chao, pp. 113-20. Taipei, Taiwan.

CLEATOR, P. E. 1959. *Lost languages.* London.

COHEN, MARCEL. 1958. *La grande invention de l'écriture et son
evolution.* Three volumes: Texte, Documentation et Index,
Planches. Paris.

COTTRELL, LEONARD. 1975. *Reading the past: The story of
deciphering ancient languages.* New York.

CROSSLAND, R. A. 1956. "Graphic linguistics and its terminology." Mechanical Translation 3/1; republished in Proceedings
of the University of Durham Philosophical Society I B (1957).

DIRINGER, DAVID. 1968. *The alphabet: A key to the history of mankind.* London and New York, 1948; 2nd edition, 1949; 3rd edition, 1968.

DOBLHOFER, ERNEST. 1957. *Voices in stone: The decipherment of ancient scripts and writings.* London and New York. [Translation of Doblhofer's *Zeichen und Wunder* (Wien, Berlin, Stuttgart, 1957).]

FÉVRIER, JAMES G. 1959. *Histoire de l'écriture.* Paris, 1948; nouvelle édition 1959.

FRANCIS, W. NELSON. 1958. *The structure of American English.* New York.

FRIEDRICH, J. 1966a. *Entzifferung verschollener Schriften und Sprachen.* Berlin, 1954; 2nd edition, 1966. [Also American and Russian editions.]

_____. 1966b. *Geschichte der Schrift, unter besonderer Berücksichtigung ihrer geistigen Entwicklung.* Heidelberg.

GELB, I. J. 1963. *A study of writing: The foundations of grammatology.* London and Chicago, 1952; revised edition, 1963. [Also editions in German, French, Italian, etc.]

_____. 1968. "Grammatology and graphemics." Papers from the Fourth Regional Meeting, Chicago Linguistic Society, ed. by Bill J. Darden, Charles-James N. Bailey, and Alice Davidson, pp. 194-201. Chicago.

_____. 1973. "Written records and decipherment." *Current trends in linguistics* 11, ed. by Thomas A. Sebeok, pp. 253-84.

_____. 1974. "Writing." Encyclopedia Britannica.

GLEASON, H. A., Jr. 1955. *An introduction to descriptive linguistics.* New York, 2nd edition, 1961.

GORDON, CYRUS H. 1968. *Forgotten scripts: How they were deciphered and their impact on contemporary culture.* New York.

HALLIDAY, M. A. K. 1961. "Categories of the theory of grammar." *Word* 17.241-92.

HOCKETT, CHARLES F. 1958. *A course in modern linguistics.* New York.

ISTRIN, V. A. 1965. *Vozniknoveniye i razvitiye pisma.* Moskva.

JENSEN, HANS. 1970. *Sign, symbol and script.* London. Translation of *Die Schrift in Vergangenheit und Gegenwart.* ed. 3, 1969.

KAHN, DAVID. 1967. *The codebreakers: The story of secret writing.* New York.

MODRZE, ANNELISE. 1930. *Zum Problem der Schrift: Ein Beitrag zur Theorie der Entzifferung.* Dissertation: Breslau.

MORRIS, CHARLES. 1946. *Signs, language, and behavior.* New York.

POPE, MAURICE. 1975. *The story of archaeological decipherment, from Egyptian Hieroglyphs to Linear B.* London and New York.

PUHVEL, J. 1975. "Epigraphy." Encyclpaedia Britannica.

READ, ALLEN W. 1948. "An account of the word 'semantic.' " *Word* 4.78-97.

SEBEOK, T. A., et al. 1964. *Approaches to semantics: Cultural anthropology, education, linguistics, psychiatry, psychology.* The Hague.

VOEGELIN, C. F. and F. M. VOEGELIN. 1961. "Typological classification of systems with included, excluded, and self-contained alphabets." *Anthropological Linguistics* 3.55-96.

_____. 1963. "Patterns of discovery in the decipherment of different types of alphabets." *American Anthropologist* 65.1231-53.

PROBLEMS OF AMERICAN INDIAN PHILOLOGY

Mary R. Haas

PROBLEMS OF AMERICAN INDIAN PHILOLOGY

Mary R. Haas

1. *Introduction.*

The study of American Indian languages is a pursuit that has been going on for more than four centuries. Within a few decades after Columbus's landing in the West Indies, the Spanish had penetrated into Mexico and Peru, and basic works on Inca (Quichua), Aymara, Nahuatl, and Tarascan—to mention only some of the earliest—were already under way. The work was done by priests, who were usually the best-educated men of their day. Far from being monolingual, they all knew Latin and Greek and many were also versed in Hebrew. They were thus as well prepared for their task as any men could be in the early part of the sixteenth century.

Throughout the intervening centuries the work of priests and missionaries, Protestant as well as Catholic, has accounted for over ninety percent of the material available on American Indian languages. This is as true of work in the twentieth century as in earlier times. But in spite of the prominent role of missionaries in this work, many other materials were collected by travellers and explorers, especially in the 17th, 18th and 19th centuries. Some of these men had very little education of any kind, while others had more sophistication in navigation, geography, and botany than in letters. But the explorer, even though he was often mainly an advance man for the exploiter, had a serious obligation to record all the information he could about rivers and mountains, flora and fauna, minerals, and other matters of possible economic importance. And included in this array of data-gathering was the obligation to provide some information about the inhabitants and their customs and languages.

By the nineteenth century some exploring expeditions were well-equipped with trained scientists to provide information on their specialty. It was unusual for linguistics, or 'philology,' as it was then often called, to be represented on an expedition; but it did happen on rare occasions. A notable instance is the case of Horatio Hale. At the age of twenty, having just been graduated from Harvard, he was appointed philologist and ethnographer to the United States Exploring Expedition, commanded by Charles Wilkes, which circumnavigated the globe from 1838 to 1842. In 1841 the Expedition stopped at the Oregon Territory and Hale departed in order to conduct a survey of the languages and peoples of Northwestern America, and he collected materials from Central California to Vancouver Island.

With the work of Hale we have come to an important turning point in the study of American Indian languages. Although his appointment was as 'philologist,' this term had a broader implication than it came to have later. He was in fact a field linguist, i.e., a scholar who wrote down linguistic information from the lips of the native speakers solely for scholarly purposes. Prior to his time (and frequently after) those who worked directly with native speakers were generally missionaries with the practical intent of translating catechisms and *confesionarios* or the Bible; while those whose interests were solely of a scholarly nature tended to rely on vocabularies, grammars, and dictionaries collected and written up by others. But Hale's work, published in 1846,[1] was not given wide circulation by the Government and did not have the impact it might otherwise have had, much to Hale's disappointment. However, Albert Gallatin, who had in 1836 published a classification of the American Indian languages of as much of North America as he had material for,[2] made good use of Hale's material in his 1848 classification which he published under the title *Hale's Indians of north-west America, and vocabularies of North America, with an introduction.*[3]

The almost complete shift from what might be called arm-chair philology, as practised by Peter S. Duponceau, Albert

[1] Horatio Hale, *Ethnography and philology. United States exploring expedition during the years 1838, 1839, 1840, 1841, 1842,* Vol. 6, ed. by Charles Wilkes. Philadelphia, 1846. Reprinted in 1968 by The Gregg Press, Inc., Ridgewood, N.J.

[2] Albert Gallatin, "A synopsis of the Indian tribes within the United States east of the Rocky Mountains and in the British and Russian possessions in North America." *Transactions and Collections of the American Antiquarian Society* 2.1-422 (1836).

[3] Albert Gallatin, *Transactions of the American Ethnological Society* 2.xxiii-clxxviii, 1-130 (1848).

Gallatin, and Robert Latham,[4] to field linguistics, as begun in the same period by men like Horatio Hale, was spurred by another exploring expedition a half century later—namely, the Jesup North Pacific Expedition of 1883-84, which initiated Franz Boas as a field anthropologist and linguist. The eventual influence of Boas was so great that through the better part of the 20th century scholarly work on American Indian languages was conducted almost entirely by the field approach. In many cases this approach became so extreme that the work of early missionaries and travellers, even where pertinent, was neglected in favor of whatever the investigator could obtain from contemporary speakers. Hence Truman Michelson, even though he had been trained in Indo-European philology in Germany under Brugmann, took the view as a field worker that "It is simply a waste of time to attempt to unravel the vagaries of the orthography of the older writers in the case of dialects existing today."[5]

This shift of emphasis had another important impact. Direct field work on American Indian languages gave rise to the descriptive method in linguistics as promulgated by Edward Sapir and Leonard Bloomfield and their immediate followers. This method finally came to be associated with what might be called an 'anti-philological' stance. This was justified on the basis of the fact that traditional orthographies often obscured the actual sounds of a language, while the use of a phonetic alphabet more often than not clarified many grammatical as well as phonological features of a language.

2. *Renewed interest in philology.*

Now, as we approach the last quarter of the 20th century, a new attitude in regard to the records of the past is gaining ascendance. The American Indian linguist is no longer exclusively a descriptive and/or comparative linguist, he is often a philologist as well; and articles are beginning to be written with this approach in mind. Indeed the volume on *Linguistics in North America*

[4]Cf. Mary R. Haas, "Grammar or lexicon? The American Indian side of the question from Duponceau to Powell." IJAL 35.239-255 (1969).

[5]Truman Michelson, "Preliminary report of the linguistic classification of Algonquian tribes." BAE-R (1906-07) 28.221-290b (1912). The quotation is from p. 280.

(*Current Trends in Linguistics,* vol. X) which has just appeared signals this new interest with an article by Ives Goddard entitled "Philological Approaches to the Study of North American Indian Languages: Documents and Documentation."[6]

American Indian philology poses all the problems of philology in general plus a few that are rather special to it. The following problems are especially deserving of study: (1) orthographies, (2) the interpretation of orthographies, (3) theoretical orientation from century to century, (4) translation, (5) extinct and unidentified languages. Within the scope of this paper most of the discussion is concerned with the first two points.

3.1. *Orthographies.*

The development of the idea of a phonetic alphabet which could be adapted to a variety of languages came rather late. Vast quantities of material on and in languages of the New World have been written in one or the other of the Euro-national orthographies—including Spanish, English, French, Portuguese, Swedish, Dutch, and German (as derivatives of the Latin alphabet), as well as Greek and Russian. Indeed for three centuries only Euronational orthographies were used, though special adaptations were of course often necessary. As might be expected, Spanish, and, more rarely, Portuguese orthographies were used in Latin America and in Florida; French, in Canada and Louisiana; while English was used in most other parts of North America, including Canada. Overlapping was common and of course travellers might make use of their national orthographies anywhere. Russian was employed in Alaska and for a few vocabularies on the coast of California. German was used by Moravian missionaries in Pennsylvania and parts of the South; and for at least one language (Creek, a Muskogean language) the Moravians are said to have adapted the Greek alphabet. Before the advent of the idea of a phonetic alphabet these orthographies were utilised, as nearly as possible, with the values they had in the language of the recorder; when new sounds had to be transcribed various kinds of adaptation had to be

---

[6]Ives Goddard, *Current Trends in Linguistics X, Linguistics in North America,* ed. by Thomas A. Sebeok, 727-745. The Hague: Mouton, 1973.

made and such adaptations might vary from recorder to recorder. Sometimes a recorder might borrow a letter or two from some other orthography known to him, as when Greek letters were sometimes employed.

In addition to the various adaptations of Euro-national orthographies in various parts of the New World, there also arose some post-Columbian native or partially native orthographies and syllabaries. Perhaps the most celebrated native syllabary is the one invented by Sequoiah for his native Cherokee. He did not understand the values of the letters of the Latin alphabet, but he was aware that white men could read by the use of such written letters. He copied letters and figures from a spelling book, sometimes backwards or upside down, and he also invented many letters. He gave each of them a syllabic value and it took him considerable time to determine how many he would need. In the end he used six symbols for each consonant sound in order to accommodate six different vowels, e.g., /ya/ /ye/ /yi/ /yo/ /yu/ /yə/. The invention of the Cherokee syllabary was an outstanding achievement.[7] It was accepted by the Cherokee leaders in 1821 and was quickly learned by dozens of previously non-literate monolingual speakers. A weekly newspaper, *The Cherokee Phoenix*, began to appear in 1828. Over the years many materials on myths, medicines, and other lore were written down by numerous Indians. Some of these have been collected and are on deposit in the Smithsonian Institution National Anthropological Archives and some have been interpreted and translated. Some have been published. But many more remain unworked and it would be hard to estimate how much material has never even been collected.

Although Moravian missionaries of the 18th century are said to have adapted the Greek alphabet for the writing of Creek, a Muskogean language of Alabama and Georgia (later Oklahoma), this method apparently did not catch on with the speakers. In the middle of the nineteenth century a collaboration between a missionary and a Creek convert led to the development of the Creek alphabet through adaptation of certain letters of the Latin

---

[7] A plate showing the characters of the Cherokee syllabary is to be found opposite p. 112 in James Mooney, "Myths of the Cherokee," BAE-R (1897-98) 19 (pt. 1) (1900).

alphabet. Since there are only thirteen consonants, little change was required. However, each consonant was always written with the same letter, unlike the practice in most European languages, and digraphs for consonants were also avoided. In addition two well-chosen adaptations were made. The letter *c* was used for the *ch* sound; and *r,* which did not occur as a phoneme of the language, was adapted for /ɬ/, the voiceless lateral spirant. The English values of the vowels and diphthongs were used, however, and this has resulted in inconsistency and ambiguity. Nevertheless, the alphabet was learned and used by large numbers of Creeks, and at one time there was a newspaper. The Bible has been written in this alphabet and there are also hymns and religious tracts. In addition there is a Creek-English and English-Creek dictionary as well as other works, such as the Constitution and Laws of the Creek Nation.

The Creek alphabet could also be adopted for use in writing some other Indian languages, and those who spoke Creek and some other Indian language often wrote both languages in the Creek alphabet. I have seen Hitchiti, another Muskogean language, and Natchez, a language isolate distantly related to Muskogean, written in this way.

Early in the nineteenth century there developed a great interest in comparing as many American Indian languages as possible in order to determine something of their interrelationships. Prominent among those who were interested in this endeavor were Benjamin Smith Barton, Thomas Jefferson, and John Pickering. But their efforts were far too often hampered in an exasperating fashion by the lack of a consistent orthography. The solution of the problem was not easy. Throughout the 19th century and on into the 20th, all kinds of recommendations were made to achieve an orthography suitable for representing the sounds of all languages. John Pickering may have been the first to tackle the problem head-on, in his essay "On the adoption of a uniform orthography for the Indian languages of North America."[8] It was successful enough to be used not only by many missionaries to the Indians but also in the Sandwich Islands. But many facts about the wide variety of sounds, especially consonants, were not yet known.

[8] John Pickering, *American Academy of Arts and Sciences—Memoirs* o.s. 4.319-360 (1818).

Interestingly enough, vowels seemed at first to be the greatest problem, not because of any great vocalic subtleties in the Indian languages, but because of the great discrepancies in the use of the familiar *a e i o u* of the Latin alphabet, especially among the English, the French, and the Germans. Pickering, recognizing the severity of this problem, recommended that these letters be used with their Italian values.

As time went on, other recommendations and modifications were made by Albert Gallatin,[9] Horatio Hale,[10] George Gibbs,[11] William Dwight Whitney,[12] and John W. Powell.[13] In spite of the great effort expended, none of these was completely satisfactory. The Powell recommendations, however, were widely used, since he required their use among the many missionaries, explorers, field workers, and Indians whom he called upon to fill out the blank Schedules he had prepared in his *Introduction to the Study of Indian Languages.*[14] The Powell alphabet, with an occasional modification, was also employed by the various field workers who were affiliated with the Bureau of American Ethnology of the Smithsonian Institution, the Bureau having been founded by Powell. These workers accumulated vast quantities of material, much of which has never been published but remains as a valuable source of information in the archives of the Bureau (now the National Anthropological Archives).

When the *Handbook of American Indian Languages,* Part 1,[15] appeared under the editorship of Franz Boas, Boas described his own orthography, which was a modification of Powell's, in his

[9]Cf. footnotes 2 and 3.

[10]Cf. footnote 1.

[11]George Gibbs, "Instructions for research relative to the ethnology and philology of America." *Smithsonian Miscellaneous Collections* 7, article 11 (= Publication 160) (1863).

[12]W. D. Whitney, "On the alphabet." *Introduction to the study of Indian languages,* by John W. Powell, 3-6. Washington, D.C., 1877.

[13]John W. Powell, *Introduction to the study of Indian languages.* 2nd ed. Washington, D.C., 1880. Contains Powell's revision of Whitney's alphabet, pp. 1-16 (see footnote 10).

[14]*Ibid.*

[15]Franz Boas, ed., *Handbook of American Indian languages,* parts 1 and 2. BAE-B 40 (1911).

"Introduction."[16] By and large, the contributors to the volume used the same general system; but if another orthography was already in use for a particular language, the editor permitted that usage, with modification if needed for phonetic accuracy. If more than one orthography was in use, equivalences might be given, as was the case for Dakota where the orthography devised by Stephen R. Riggs was preferred but the equivalents in the system devised by James O. Dorsey are also presented.[17]

But there was a growing dissatisfaction with some of the deficiencies of the system as well as with some of the more awkward symbols being used, such as the exclamation point to mark glottalized consonants (e.g., *p! t! k!*) or the raised epsilon ᵉ to indicate the glottal stop. Consequently some of the members of the American Anthropological Association, among them Franz Boas and Edward Sapir, sponsored a revised orthography. This was explained and illustrated in "Phonetic Transcription of Indian Languages," published in 1916.[18] This system of transcription rather quickly superseded earlier systems. This means, for instance, that Sapir's transcription of a particular language would be given in one system of transcription before 1916 and in the revised system after that date. Many linguists gave no more clue as to the change than to say after 1916, "The alphabet is that now in general use in America."[19]

As will be readily understood, the problems encountered in finding an orthography for American Indian languages are no different from those encountered with other unwritten languages. But the orthographic traditions of North America were little affected by what went on in other parts of the world. About this

[16]Franz Boas, "Introduction." *Handbook of American Indian languages,* part 1. BAE-B 40.1-83 (1911). Reprinted (with J. W. Powell, *Indian linguistic families of America north of Mexico*), Lincoln, Nebraska: University of Nebraska Press, 1966. Parts reprinted in *Language in culture and society: A reader in linguistics and anthropology,* ed. by Dell Hymes, 15-26, 121-123. New York, Evanston and London: Harper and Row, 1964.

[17]Franz Boas and John R. Swanton, "Siouan (Dakota)." *Handbook of American Indian languages,* part 1. BAE-B 40.875-965 (1911).

[18]Franz Boas, E. Sapir, P. E. Goddard, and A. L. Kroeber, "Phonetic transcription of Indian languages." *Smithsonian Miscellaneous Collections* 66(6) (1916).

[19]Pliny E. Goddard, "Wailaki texts." IJAL 2.77-137 (1921). The quotation is on p. 77.

time a group of European scholars founded the International Phonetic Association, and one of the first things they did was to devise a standardized orthography which they called the International Phonetic Alphabet, or IPA.[20] Although this alphabet would have been useful for American Indian languages, its use did not catch on among American linguists who seemed inclined to stick with their own system. One of the few field workers who did use it (other than an occasional visiting European) was John P. Harrington, who in spite of having been taken on as an ethnologist in the Bureau of American Ethnology, which had usually been rather conservative in its orthographic usage, made some use of the IPA in some of his work. However, he also used many idiosyncratic signs of his own invention, as in his *Kiowa Vocabulary*.[21]

So, except for a few deviants like Harrington, the A.A.A. system was more or less consistently applied for the next quarter of a century. By the early 1930's, however, certain ideas about the theory of the phoneme were developing and some changes were again in order. In 1934, a group of six Yale linguists published a note in the *American Anthropologist* entitled "Some Orthographic Recommendations"[22] which set forth some very important changes. These were accepted more readily and more widely than any previous recommendations among American Indian linguists. Some influence of the IPA could be seen but in general the system retained many important distinctions. After forty years this orthographic system is still widely used though quite a few individual variations have crept in, particularly in the last decade.

These 1934 orthographic recommendations had a strong impact in two ways. The first was the dictum that "A suitable orthography for representing the sounds of a given language should provide a unit symbol for each phoneme, i.e., for each psychologically unitary sound. . . ."[23] The second impact was the

[20] See, for example, *The principles of the International Phonetic Association*. London: International Phonetic Association, 1949.

[21] John P. Harrington, "Vocabulary of the Kiowa language." BAE-B 84 (1928).

[22] George Herzog, Stanley S. Newman, Edward Sapir, Mary Haas Swadesh, Morris Swadesh and Charles F. Voegelin, "Some orthographic recommendations arising out of discussions by a group of six American linguists." AA 36.629-631 (1934).

[23] *Ibid.*, p. 629.

abandonment of certain idiosyncrasies that had characterized the Americanist system for many decades. The most perturbing of these was the use of *c* for the sound of English *sh*. I do not know who first used this letter in this way but it has been found in the writings of missionaries of French Canada belonging to the middle of the 19th century. It is undeniable that the selection of a proper symbol for this sound has almost always been controversial and the proper interpretation of the multiplicity of representations that are or have been in use requires not a little esoteric knowledge. The 1934 recommendation was to use [š]. Most of the other changes involved the adaptation or invention of unitary symbols for the former digraphs; e.g., [c] for *ts*, [č] for *tc*, [λ] for *dl* and [ƛ] for *tł*. The general adoption of these recommendations was rather swift. Articles employing them began to appear in the *International Journal of American Linguistics*, in *Language*, and elsewhere. Languages like Nootka (Vancouver Island), which had been worked on by Edward Sapir from the early part of the century, were written in one orthography before 1916, in another orthography after 1916, and in still another after 1934. The change in the value of the letter *c* has been a particular source of misunderstanding, especially since *c* is often also used for [č] if only one affricate occurs in a given language.

Within the last decade or so there has come to be less uniformity among linguists in orthographic use than formerly, but for the most part the variations are individual. Thus in writing his Athapaskan materials Harry Hoijer used the digraph *tł* prior to 1934, ƛ for a couple of decades after 1934, and then readopted the old Boasian *L* in an article in 1960,[24] and has also sometimes returned to the digraph *tł*. Similar vacillations could be cited for other writers.

The major change that has taken place in the last decade is the influence of recent phonological theory. Here the phoneme of the 1930s is bypassed; an underlying form is formulated and a sequence of rules derives the phonetic output. The actual phonetic symbols used for this last stage, however, have not necessarily undergone much change. But when words are written morphophonemically rather than phonetically, a particular language

[24] Harry Hoijer, "Athapaskan languages of the Pacific coast." *Culture in history: Essays in honor of Paul Radin,* ed. by Stanley Diamond, 960-976. New York: Columbia University Press, 1960.

can present an utterly different appearance from what it had when written according to classical phonemic theory.

3.2. *Problems in the interpretation of the writing system.*

With four centuries of accumulated materials, with numerous Euro-national orthographies and specially adapted orthographies (such as for Creek), and the even more numerous phonetic orthographies, any would-be philologist who wishes to make use of a given document (even a short vocabulary) soon realizes that he must have a great deal of information before he can make a phonetic interpretation of it. The chief kinds of additional information needed can be summarized as follows:

Up to 1800 it is necessary to know the nationality of the recorder in order to interpret his orthographic usage. Contrast, for example, the value of *ch* in Spanish and English, in French, and in German; or the value of *j* in Spanish, in English, in French, and in German; etc.

From 1800 on it is still often necessary to know the nationality of the recorder, but it is also necessary to know whether he has adopted one of the standardized phonetic orthographies that begin to appear every generation or so. And after 1900 it may be very important to know whether the document was written before or after 1916, before or after 1934, and so on. For example, if a student working on Algonkian equates *c* written by Bloomfield in 1925[25] with *c* written by him in 1946[26] (as has been done in more than one instance), he has made a serious error.

The orthography of the document may be one especially invented or adapted for the particular language, and the letters may very well have quite idiosyncratic values; e.g., *r* for [ł] in Creek.

[25] Leonard Bloomfield, "On the sound system of Central Algonquian." *Language* 1.130-156 (1925).

[26] Leonard Bloomfield, "Algonquian." *Linguistic structures of native America*, by Harry Hoijer and others (Viking Fund Publications in Anthropology 6), 85-129 (1946). Reprinted with corrections, *A Leonard Bloomfield anthology*, ed. by Charles F. Hockett, 440-488. Bloomington and London: Indiana University Press, 1970.

The occupation of the recorder may also be very important since it may give a clue to his degree of education or to the amount of time he may have spent listening to the language. Thus vocabularies written down by travellers, explorers, or surveyors may be based on just a few hours' work— not enough time to grasp the sounds of a strange language other than superficially, even for a linguist. Anthropologists may also spend very little time on the language, while those who do spend considerable time can probably be counted as linguists. Then we have missionaries and linguists who generally spend a considerable amount of time with a language and we can thus hope we have a more reliable document.

The preceding points are based on the assumption that the recorder is a foreigner. We also have many documents written by native speakers (e.g., Cherokees, Creeks, Choctaws, Dakotas, and many others), where a certain amount of literacy may have become rather general in the tribe. A somewhat different situation exists when a single native speaker has been taught to write his language in order to provide material for the linguist, as when Sapir taught Alex Thomas to write Nootka. In either of these cases carelessness in regard to certain features, especially diacritics, may develop, as when most Creeks dropped the macron on $\bar{e}$ (to be read [i·]) and it could not be distinguished from e (to be read [i]).

It is also necessary to know the theoretical orientation of the period in which the document was written; in times of fluctuation it is even necessary to know the theoretical orientation of the person writing the document. A document prepared in terms of classical phonemic theory will require a very different interpretation from one written prior to the development of the theory. Sapir's early Nootka materials contain a wealth of phonetic detail, including whispered vowels and consonantal timbres as well as variant recordings of one and the same word; but the phonemically transcribed materials published later lack these details and variations.[27]

[27]Edward Sapir, "The rival whalers, a Nitinat story (Nootka text with translation and grammatical analysis)." IJAL 3.76-102 (1924-25); Edward Sapir and Morris Swadesh, *Nootka texts: Tales and ethnological narratives with grammatical notes and lexical materials.* Special Publication of the Linguistic Society of America. Philadelphia, 1939.

If the language of the document is extinct but has living relatives, guidance in the phonetic interpretation of the document can be gained (though not without pitfalls) through comparison with modern dialects.

If the language of the document is extinct and has no known relatives, the chances of making some determination of the sounds represented range from very poor to reasonable, depending upon the various factors mentioned above.

Examples of some of the problems mentioned above may help clarify some points. Not all of the priests who followed the Spanish conquerors into Mexico and Peru were Spanish-born—some may have been Italian or Portuguese. And even though they might still adopt Spanish orthography in writing an Indian language, their hearing of the new sounds would be influenced by their native language.

There is an even more serious problem in regard to documents written in Spanish possessions in the 16th century. Spanish of this period was undergoing some sound changes and for this reason, if the value of the Indian sound is unknown, the interpretation can be extremely troublesome since it may be impossible to determine which side of the sound shift the recorder's speech is on. This problem causes difficulties in the interpretation of the many 16th century documents of Mexico and Peru. Fortunately many of these languages are still spoken so it is usually possible to make plausible deductions. However, it is not all smooth sailing even then, and this for two reasons: (1) the modern dialect may not be a direct descendant of the 16th century recorded dialect; and (2) in four hundred years the Indian language may have undergone some sound shifts.

There is a tremendous amount of philological work that could be done in comparing these early recorded languages with their modern descendants and/or relatives, but the surface has scarcely been scratched, largely because the philological frame of reference has been so widely neglected by American Indian linguists, as I have mentioned earlier.

In 1950 John H. Rowe made a preliminary attack on such a problem in his article "Sound Patterns in Three   Inca

Dialects"[28] by using the modern Cuzco and Ayacucho dialects to make a detailed determination of the sounds of Classic Inca. The problem of the sibilants, however, was not completely solved, as he explains:

> Examining the distributions of the letters *s, ss, ç,* and *z* in our documents we find that they fall easily into pairs. . . . It seems likely, then, that these four letters represent a maximum of two phonemes; the question is whether there really were two such phonemes in the Classic dialect or whether the four letters represent merely an extension of obsolete spelling conventions to Inca. In the latter case we might have only one *s* phoneme as in modern Cuzco and Ayacucho.[29]

Now we are faced here with a most remarkable set of circumstances. Clearly we need more Spanish philological studies to determine more about the 16th century variant spellings and pronunciations. At the same time there is a considerable amount of 16th century material written in Aymara and several languages of Mexico which could be subjected to the same kind of philological analysis as has been applied to Inca by Rowe. Moreover, I venture to say that if this were properly done, American Indian philology might possibly throw some light on 16th century Spanish philology. In this way important new possibilities could be opened up in the future. The chief difficulty is that a great many Indian specialists would have to get involved and then their work would have to be made known to and understood by Hispanic philologists.[30]

Similar philological problems exist in the interpretation of all of the other Euro-national orthographies. Indeed most of them pose even more problems than the Spanish. The worst of all is probably the English, though French can be pretty exasperating, and while the chief use of these two orthographies was in the 17th, 18th and early 19th centuries, some use has continued to the

[28]John H. Rowe. IJAL 16.137-148 (1950).

[29]*Ibid.,* p. 146.

[30]John Rowe has informed me of some work done along these lines. See, for example, William J. Entwistle, *The Spanish language, together with Portuguese, Catalan and Basque.* London: Faber and Faber, 1936. The section on pp. 246-7 is titled "American Indian evidence for the evolution of Spanish."

present. French missionaries of the 17th and 18th centuries prepared a large volume of material on the Iroquoian and Algonkian languages, and much of this material remains unpublished. Victor E. Hanzeli provides much valuable information in "Missionary Linguistics in New France,"[31] including a discussion of the way in which the missionaries worked and a list of many of the unpublished manuscripts.

Many more examples could be adduced but these will suffice for the present. There remain a few more points in regard to writing which deserve some discussion.

3.3. *Miscopying.*

Miscopying is as serious a problem in American Indian philology as it is elsewhere. It is especially critical in the case of extinct languages. When handwritten vocabularies are published in printed form, all sorts of errors creep in. Even an experienced linguist may have no way of figuring out whether a particular squiggle is to be interpreted as *wi, we, mi, me, nu, un, im, iin,* or whatever, and it is not hard to find examples of this. And when an amateur prepares a handwritten vocabulary for publication, the results can be almost useless. This would not be too bad if users would only remember the high likelihood of error, but there is a tendency to overlook this. I know of no way around this except by publishing a facsimile of the original manuscript alongside the printed interpretation. The reader then has a chance to make his own interpretation of the handwriting and to make corrections accordingly. A good example of this having been done is seen in John P. Harrington's "The original Strachey vocabulary of the Virginia Indian language."[32] Although Harrington has considerable familiarity with Algonkian languages, he has made some errors of interpretation. These can often be corrected by referring to the facsimile, particularly if the word has cognates. For example, where Harrington reads *Quautamu,* I read *Quantamu,* which is from Proto-Algonkian **kwantamwa* 'he swallows it.' In place of

---

[31] Victor E. Hanzeli. Janua Linguarum, series major 29. The Hague: Mouton, 1969.

[32] John P. Harrington. BAE-B 167.189-202 (= Anthropological Paper 46) (1955).

Racaioh 'sand,' I read *Racawh*, which is from PA **le·kawi.* But to publish all such things in facsimile would be very expensive, so it must be emphasized that when a facsimile is not given the original should be checked by the user whenever possible.

There is another kind of miscopying which can very easily be overlooked by the American Indian philologist. This arises from the copying and recopying of the same document through many hands. In this case it may even be very difficult to determine which is the original. This problem can arise at any time, of course, but it is particularly to be remembered in connection with materials from the first half of the nineteenth century. This was the time when interest was high in obtaining vocabularies of as many American Indian languages as possible in order to attempt to classify them. Interested persons traded copies of such vocabularies and there is often no knowing how many handwritten copies exist, with no one knows how many errors in each. Thomas Jefferson, Peter S. Duponceau, Albert Gallatin, Robert Latham, and many others were engaged in this activity.

There is still another kind of miscopying which arises to plague us. This is when a field worker makes a mistake in copying his own notes, either because he is unable at times to read his own handwriting or through an occasional lapse. Many of the field workers of the Bureau of American Ethnology would make a 'fair copy' of their original field notes. Sometimes the original was then destroyed, but at other times both copies are still extant. After the typewriter came into use, the fair copy was often made on the typewriter. If the typewritten copy had no errors, it was an improvement since it eliminated undecipherable squiggles. But the greatest chance for error arises when a field worker transcribes his original notes into another phonetic system. Since phonetic orthographies tend to change every twenty or thirty years, there is scarcely a field worker who has not had to do just this. When the same letter is used with different values in succeeding systems, the chances for error are very great.

3.4. *Rewriting.*

By 'rewriting' I mean not simply transcribing a document from one phonetic system into another, but a reinterpretation of the writing system of the original document. This problem arose particularly during the time when many linguists wished to reinterpret older works in terms of phonemic theory. In many cases this simply cannot be done with satisfactory results. But the temptation can be very strong, especially in the case of materials written with a plethora of phonetic niceties which are so difficult to print and awkward to quote. It is really not possible to be dogmatic about whether rewriting should be done or not be done. There may be occasions when it can serve a useful purpose. But it is always risky, especially in the case of extinct languages, and so probably should be avoided if possible. A good example occurs in the case of Ofo, a Siouan language of the Southeast. The only vocabulary we have of the language was taken down by John R. Swanton early in this century.[33] He frequently wrote *x, x̣,* or *h* after certain consonants but sometimes he wrote the same word without such indication. Although he himself was at pains to point out that "*x, x̣,* and *h* all usually stand for the aspirate which follows several Siouan consonants and is particularly prominent in the Ofo language,"[34] several Siouanists have chosen to rewrite his words without any indication of aspiration. But careful comparison with Siouan languages west of the Mississippi shows this to be a mistake. Ofo aspirated consonants must be recognized as phonemes distinct from unaspirated consonants even though Biloxi and Tutelo, its nearest relatives, lack the distinction, for the Ofo aspirated consonants correspond to both aspirated and glottalized consonants of Dakota. In terms of Proto-Siouan we discover that Ofo *t* is from PS *$*t$ or *$*r$ while Ofo *th* (or *tx, tx̣*) is from PS *$*th$ or *$*tʔ$. Thus we have PS *$*topa$ 'four.' Ofo *toʼpa*; PS *$*thá$ 'ruminant,' Ofo *iʼtxa* 'deer'; PS *$*tʔéhi$ 'to die,' Ofo *a̱thẽʼ*.[35]

4. *Conclusion.*

Although I have tried to sketch out the multiplicity of orthographic problems through four centuries and a wide variety of languages of the New World, there are doubtless many things that

[33]J. O. Dorsey and John R. Swanton, "A dictionary of the Biloxi and Ofo languages." BAE-B 47 (1912).

[34]*Ibid.,* p. 319.

[35]Mary R. Haas, "Swanton and the Biloxi and Ofo dictionaries." IJAL 35.286-290 (1969).

have not been touched upon. As the awareness of philological problems among these languages grows we shall see many kinds of specialties arise. With some languages there is enough material to concentrate on one language (including perhaps its dialects) through several centuries, as could be done with Kechua (Quichua or Inca), Aymara, Nahuatl, or Yucatec, for example. In other cases there is material for specialization in a language family, such as Algonkian, which has many living representatives but also great quantities of older materials on languages which have long disappeared, as well as some which are still spoken. Or one could specialize in a certain tradition, such as Spanish missionaries in the 16th century or French missionaries in the 17th century, or Moravian missionaries of the 18th century, or even Summer Institute of Linguistics missionaries of the 20th century. Clearly a wealth of possibilities lies ahead and the whole field of the study of American Indian languages will profit thereby.

GREEK VOCABULARY AND THE CHRISTIANS

Reinhold Merkelbach

GREEK VOCABULARY AND THE CHRISTIANS

Reinhold Merkelbach

1. *Introduction.*

My subject will be the transformation of Greek vocabulary which occurred when the Greek world became Christian. The language people spoke remained grammatically unchanged, but their thoughts had become different, and the meaning of many words altered drastically. Christians often changed the sense of traditional words so as to fit their concepts, and some semantic areas took on entirely new meanings. Such processes of semantic revaluation take place in every changing society.

There are various reasons why the meaning of words should change. One had to use words already available to describe the new Christian reality, and through slight changes of nuance it became possible to express Christian ideas with them. This is a perfectly commonplace process. But there were also words which were used to describe generally recognized values, but which at the same time had close associations with the pagan world that the Christians wanted to overcome: such words as *aretê* 'virtue, excellence, ability, success,' *andreia* 'boldness, manliness,' *enkrateia* 'self-control, temperance.' It would have been quite impossible to give up these words: a person who did not himself strive after *aretê* 'virtue' could hardly have attempted missionary activities among the Hellenes. It was therefore necessary that Christians too strive after *aretê* 'virtue,' even though the Hellenic manner of striving for *aretê* 'virtue *and success*' was not easily compatible with Christian humility. The Christians accordingly gave *aretê* a Christian meaning which differed in its nuances from the Hellenic sense of the word. Contemporaries might believe that when Christians spoke of their 'virtue' they meant the same *aretê* that everyone knew, but in reality the Christian nuance gave the word almost a new meaning. Moreover, there were words that were used in the suppression and refutation of Christianity—the words used in the amphitheatre where the martyrs were killed, and the philosophic words used by pagan writers to show the simplicity of Christian teaching. They were the really dangerous ones. Simply to ignore them would not have done; the only successful course was to use them oneself, but to give them a new twist and use them as weapons against the pagans.

I shall comment on three groups of words which the Christians adopted and changed in their characteristic way—words from political life, from sport, and from philosophy. With the political words one can show how the Christians at first totally rejected the worldly state, the Roman Empire, and strove to obtain citizenship not in this world but in heaven. On the other hand they took over certain political concepts from the Greeks, and particularly from Greek democracy. Consequently, certain democratic elements rooted themselves firmly in Christianity, which never became a totally hierarchical religious community.

On words from Greek sport one could speak at considerable length. The language of sport was carried over in the Imperial age to the combat of men and animals in the amphitheatre; Christian martyrs also died in the amphitheatre, and this was the place where the battle between the Roman Empire and the new religion took place. The pagan onlooker regarded gladiatorial combat from the standpoint of a Roman citizen; the point of view of the Christian victim was something quite different. So the Romans and Christians spoke about the same reality, and the antagonistic parties used the same words, but they used them with different meanings and quite different moral values.

Finally, we shall examine some words from Greek philosophy. The Christians would have had no chance of winning Greek converts to their new religion if they had not reached the intellectual level of pagan philosophers and opposed pagan philosophy with their own Christian philosophy, that is, with theology. It was no easy task. Greek philosophical vocabulary was precise, an admirable tool for its subject. Pagan philosophers such as Celsus and Porphyry used it to combat Christianity. The Christian philosophers, above all Clement and Origen, twisted this weapon around; they used Greek pagan concepts to support their own ideas and to prove the truth of the Christian faith. But in this way Christianity was also thoroughly penetrated by the concepts of Greek philosophy. Of course, many philosophical words took on quite new meanings in the course of this process. At the end of this paper I shall present some selected examples of this.

2. *Political words.*

Among the political words, one may mention 'liturgy, polity, ekklesia, episkopos (bishop), synedrion, synod, dogma.' I shall comment briefly upon all of them.

In earlier Greek, 'liturgy' had meant 'service for the people': a liturgy consisted of building a ship for the city's fleet or taking over the costs for a theatrical production. But then in Hellenistic times the word took on a religious meaning in the cult of the Greeks and among the Jews: 'services for the community of the faithful,' 'service for god.' Thus in the Imperial age there were two meanings of the word at the same time: 'liturgy' usually meant a task which a well-to-do citizen accepted upon order from the state; but it was also possible to use the word in religious connections. The Christians took over this second usage alone, and dropped the civic meaning.

The word *politeia* 'polity' in ancient Greek means 'constitution,' sometimes equivalent to 'democracy.' This word in Christian texts means 'way of life.' The 'right way of life' consists of self-control, not merely physical, but also spiritual. The Christian *politeia* meant 'asceticism'; *politeuesthai* can actually mean 'to fast'; and *politeutes* 'citizen, councilman' is for the Christian a man who lives ascetically and piously.

The Christian community was called *ekklêsia*. That is the Greek word for 'assembly of the people': the Jews had already used the word in the Hellenistic period for their own communities, which were at once religious and political. Since the Christians conceived of themselves as a new nationality that had taken its place beside the older peoples of the world, the designation *ekklêsia* for their new, purely religious gatherings was only suitable; and yet the content of this 'popular assembly' was something entirely fresh. In these Christian 'popular assemblies,' officials were elected by a count of raised hands, just as in the popular assemblies of the Greeks. Such a procedure seems only natural to us, but that was by no means the case at that time. Voting was not a common device among the peoples of the ancient Near East, such as the Persians, Assyrians, or Egyptians. Voting is characteristic of Greek and Roman democracy. In the Christian Church, such voting remained in practice to some degree at every period.

The most important church office was that of 'overseer' *episkopos,* the bishop—again a Greek word. The Athenians and Rhodians had elected such 'overseers,' *episkopoi,* as democratic officials for various duties. Here, then, we have a political concept of the Greek city which has become the designation for a religious office.

The 'council meeting' of the presbyters is called *synhedrion* by Ignatius. The word was already in use among the Jews of the age of Jesus. The local council in the Roman province Judaea was called the *Sanhedrin*—a Greek loanword. In Greece the council of, for example, the Amphiktyons in Delphi, was called *synhedrion;* and the representatives of the states who came together for the Second Athenian League, or celebrated the festival of Athena Ilias in Ilion, were called *synedroi.*

Another Greek name for a political assembly that met to consider and draw up resolutions was *synodos* 'synod, council.' When a Greek assembly drew up a resolution, this was called a *dogma.* Such resolutions were drawn up, e.g., by the Amphiktyonic Council, by the assembly of the Second League of Athens, by the people of Rhodes, and by the Roman Senate. The words 'council' and 'dogma,' then, have a surprisingly democratic background. I must add that the history of the word *dogma* is complicated. The philosophers of the Hellenistic period had used the term, and meant thereby a statement which they considered to be accurate. We shall return to this point later.

One may conclude that the Christians took over for the internal organization of their communities words and forms that sprang from Greek democracy. They often gave these words a rather different meaning, as in the case of *dogma* and *synodos;* but they could not set aside the old meanings altogether, for with the words they had also adopted a part of the old institutions. And so there came into Church organization essentially democratic elements which always remained a healthy counterweight against the hierarchical structure to which the Church of late antiquity and the medieval period turned. This surely contributed to the strength and resistance of the exterior 'body' of the Church; for an organization can be strong only if it has support at the lower levels, not if it is governed exclusively by orders from on high. One may suppose that the Church owed this internal resistance in large part to the concepts and institutions which it adopted from the democratic *polis.*

3. *Greek Athletics, Gladiatorial Combats, and the Imperial Cult.*

The second group of words to be taken into consideration comes from Greek athletics. When one begins to study these words in the earlier Christian texts, one is amazed at their frequency. The vocabulary of Greek sports is very rich and technical, and yet almost all of it has been transferred into the language of the Christians. I can give but a brief sketch of this. Let us consider the words 'ascetic, athlete, agonistes.'

The word 'ascetic' was originally applied to athletes in training. *Askeo* means 'train.' An athlete in training had to lead a regular life, to eat neither too much nor too little, to drink no wine, to abstain from love-making and to carry out his exercises every day, even in the hottest weather. It was because of this association of the word that Greek philosophers, especially Epictetus, spoke of having 'to train oneself' to lead the proper life. The Christians then gave the word a whole new value: it designated the Christian athlete—the martyr, and the monk who chastises himself in the desert, abstains from all the pleasures of life, and carries on a pitiless war with his own body.

This process of revaluation affected the word *athlêtês* as well. A martyr or monk is likewise a Christian 'athlete.' The same thing happened with the word *agônistês* 'combatant.' Milton's *Samson Agonistes* is such a combatant for the faith.

Such revaluations are characteristic. Gymnasium and sports were the very center of Greek life. A young man had to strive for excellence, to choose the rough way, to compete, to toil, and to sweat, in order to become prominent among his fellow citizens here on earth. Now Christianity denied and negated this entire form of life from its very foundations. The Christian does not try to distinguish himself through competition with others, but, if at all, through humility. And he strives not for happiness on earth, but for blessedness in heaven. When the Church became the State religion, the gymnasia were closed and the athletic festivals abolished. Originally, they had been festivals of pagan gods, and the gymnasia were places where one enjoyed one's body and the world. Given the Christian opposition to things worldly, all this was quite unacceptable. Christianity discarded the idea that competition should play a central role in human life, and rejected the life of the Greek city, the *polis*; it strove for the *civitas dei.* The

Christians wanted nothing to do with sports, with the cult of the body; but they used the vocabulary of Greek sports metaphorically for their new concepts, for the Christian ascetics and combatants for the faith, above all for the martyrs. While the Greek athletes had striven for the laurel crown in the Olympic games, Christian martyrs endured in order to win the never-fading, the amaranthine crown in heaven. To them, the prize was not awarded by earthly umpires, but by God himself.

But to understand fully the revaluation of the Greek sports vocabulary, one must also take into account another phenomenon, the gladiatorial and animal combats. In the time of the Roman Empire, the gladiatorial fights were introduced into the Greek lands. The combats were enacted in the amphitheatre, and the whole vocabulary of Greek sports was transferred to these shows. These spectacles were not merely expressions of a cruel temper; they were part of the Roman imperial cult. We do not find them otherwise. It would seem that they were occasions to demonstrate impressively that the Emperor was the master of life and death. So it came to pass that among the Romans, at narrowly limited periods, the priest of the Emperor in a province would put on gladiatorial shows.

Now the Christians consistently refused the pledges of loyalty to the Emperor, pledges which to the other inhabitants of the empire seemed quite harmless. But the Christians denied the legitimacy of worldly authorities on principle. So it was by no means chance or accident that the clash between Christianity and the Empire took place in the amphitheatre, for this was the site of the ruler cult, and the ruler cult was precisely the question at stake. The Romans tried to enforce the recognition of the Empire by putting to death in public spectacles those people who would not profess loyalty. This was intended as a deterrent example. The Christians, on the other hand, felt that the slain brethren actually were not victims, but victors in these shows, and that they served as edifying and comforting examples. They took the fine-sounding athletic words, which to the Greeks and Romans had indicated a whole way of life, and forged them into weapons that could be used against the Roman state.

The Christian church, it should be admitted, was a kind of anti-state within the Empire. The Christians did not recognize the legitimacy of the rulers; they appropriated the concepts and the language of the Romans, giving the words a new twist. They were a separate community with its own language. When Constantine sought a pretext to set himself up against his fellow-rulers and to take all power into his own hand, then this anti-state, the Christian Church, offered itself as a pretext and tool. After his victory, he made Christianity the state religion. In the same century, all vanished together—Imperial cult, gladiatorial combat, and Greek sport.

4. *Philosophical words.*

Finally, the Christians took over thoughts and concepts from pagan philosophy. This was done abundantly, in order to build up gradually a 'Christian philosophy,' that is, that structure of teachings which we call theology. As in philosophy, so also in theology, men tried through precise definitions to create a firm basis on which one could build further; and in theology as in philosophy the aim was to work up from this firm basis, and by means of logical conclusions achieve a complete and coherent system of thought. This procedure had regrettable consequences; for the philosophical concepts and methods were used not as tools to achieve real understanding but as a means of argumentation in the service of theology; and philosophy was thereby degraded to a mere handmaiden to theology (*ancilla theologiae*). We want to show with a few selected examples how the philosophical concepts of the Greeks were taken over and altered by Christian authors.

orthê doxa and *epistêmê.*

The Platonic theory of knowledge states that men bring with them many opinions from a former life; among these are true and correct opinions (*alêtheis, orthai doxai*), but also false ones. It is of the greatest practical importance to determine how one can distinguish the true from the false opinions. It can only be accomplished by testing them; in the course of the testing one can find criteria for determining which opinions are correct. One must discover the causes of observable relationships, for when one has determined the causes of a given phenomenon, then one can determine which of one's opinions were correct and which were false. The correct ones are then no longer merely non-binding 'opinions,' but become firm foundations, knowledge (*epistêmê*).

Thus 'right opinions' are non-binding and of little value, since at first one cannot distinguish them from the false ones. One hesitates to decide, and then it can easily come about that the right opinion escapes again. One must therefore test his opinions and so gain understanding; when one knows the causes and can formulate them, then one has achieved 'knowledge,' and knowledge is of great value. It stands on a higher level than the non-binding 'right opinion.'

It is clear that orthodoxy, 'right opinion,' in the Christian authors, is a caricature of the Platonic theory of recognition, for here 'right opinion' is elevated into a firm value. Now the important thing is to hold firm to right opinion; there is no longer any possibility of testing this or any other view. What Plato characterized as fluid and relatively trivial is now supposed to serve as the fundamental groundwork of a philosophical system.

In Plato what one could establish firmly was called 'knowledge' *epistêmê,* and it enjoyed a far higher rank than 'right opinion.' If, then, in the language of Christian theology 'right opinion' had already become the firm ground on which one can (and must) stand fast, then where is 'knowledge' *epistêmê*? Obviously it must stand even higher than orthodoxy, because that is required by the traditional ranking of the philosophical ideas. But what ranks higher than orthodoxy? Well, above orthodoxy, which is available for everyone in its fixed formulations, stands the individual, intuitive knowledge of God, the half-ecstatic submersion in God, from which a religious person can find a much firmer and more certain basis for his faith than any orthodoxy can provide. One can say, and rightly, that such intuitive knowledge ranks far above orthodoxy, and yet is really the basis on which orthodoxy is built. The word *epistêmê* and also *gnôsis* now designate the intuitive knowledge of God.

But here we have a complete reversal of the meanings of the words. Platonic knowledge was based on the recognition and formulation of causes; Christian knowledge, on intuition. It therefore remained vague and unsteady. Theological argumentation was possible, if at all, only in the realm of orthodoxy, of right opinion; in the higher realm of knowledge it no longer had a place, for shaky intuition stood superior to firm orthodoxy, whereas in Plato firm knowledge had stood superior to shaky opinion. The words had so drastically altered their meanings that the 'knowledge' of the Christians is no longer a knowledge which can be supported by reason.

I should like to stress that the Christian theological system is in many ways admirably suited to its subject. There can be no doubt that in religion intuition and religious sensibility really do stand superior to orthodoxy. Here we wish merely to point out that the Christians took over two concepts of the Platonic theory of knowledge and gave them new meanings that were directly opposed to the old ones.

dogma and *hairesis.*

We have already met the word *dogma* in speaking of political words; it designated the 'resolution' of a popular assembly or council. Such resolutions were not regarded as being in principle equivalent to law, but in practice they often had the same force. One can also translate *dogma* as 'that which was found pleasing,' 'that which seems good.' The word is also found in the language of philosophy. There *dogma* means a statement which pleased some given philosopher, seemed right to him, and was used by him as a foundation for his further thought. So there are *dogmata* of the Stoics or the Epicureans, and the entire philosophy of these schools is composed of such *dogmata* or philosophic precepts. Within one system many *dogmata* are needed, because one precept is built upon the preceding; when one precept falls, then usually a section of the system collapses at the same time. But naturally the *dogmata* of the philosophers could lay no claim to exclusive validity since there were many schools existing side by side, each with different *dogmata.*

The word *hairesis* is derived from *haireô* 'choose'; we find it in those passages which describe how a man makes a decision that affects the rest of his life. In daily use, *hairesis* can mean a 'group, division,' as of a group of young men in the gymnasium which one could join voluntarily. In Hellenistic Greece *hairesis* often designated a philosophic group or 'sect.' A young man had the 'choice' of joining the Academy, the Peripatetics, the Stoics, the Epicureans, and the choice of a 'sect' determined at least partly his future way of life. The man who chose a *hairesis* naturally also chose the *dogmata,* the precepts or the teachings connected with it. So in Greek philosophy a whole series of 'sects, groups, parties' *haireseis* stood one beside the other, and each had its own 'precepts' *dogmata.* The word was also adopted by the Jews. The Sadducees and Pharisees were *haireseis* within the Jewish religion, and Christianity was called 'the *hairesis* of the Nazarenes.'

The Christians too took over these words *hairesis* and *dogma,* They had sects just as the Greeks, Egyptians, and Jews did, and these sects had their characteristic precepts, *dogmata.* But this pluralism did not last long. Only that *dogma,* that precept, was considered valid which was orthodox; other precepts were the opinion of the heterodox. In the long run, the Church had no place for groups of different opinion. The Christian meanings of the words *hairesis* and *dogma* were obviously modelled after the schools of Hellenistic philosophy. But here too the linguistic practice of the Christians brought about a drastic change in the sense of both words, simply through the fact that there was no longer a series of groups with various precepts, but one single group with its dogmatic system which alone was considered valid.

pistis.

The Greek verb *peithô* is to our way of thinking ambiguous, for it means 'persuade' as well as 'convince.' The related substantive *pistis* has a correspondingly ambiguous meaning: it can mean 'conviction, trust,' and it may well happen that one is deceived in this trust; but *pistis* can also mean 'guarantee, demonstration, proof.'

Now the Christians designated their religious faith, their religion, in which they placed their trust, with the word *pistis.* When one analyses carefully the use Christian thinkers make of the word *pistis* 'faith,' it can easily be shown that they constantly mix up different things which can, however, equally be denoted by the word *pistis.* They say, e.g., that nothing can be surer than 'demonstration'; for this concept they use the word *pistis.* Then they go on pretending to have demonstrated that the Christian faith—again, the word *pistis*—is beyond any doubt. Even Clement, elsewhere always a very clear thinker, displays a shocking lack of precision in the constantly changing nuances of the word *pistis.* An unobservant reader could easily be convinced that *pistis* 'faith' provided a very solid foundation for the teaching of God, because all *pistis,* according to the basic meaning of the word, implies proof.

homoiôsis.

Plato taught that men ought to try to be as god-like in life as is humanly possible. The Christian Platonists took this central bit of Greek philosophy into their own system. They found support for this in that passage of Genesis (1: 26) where God speaks to Himself, "Let us make man in our form and image," *poiêsômen anthrôpon kat' eikona hêmeteran kai kath' homoiôsin.* Here the Jews, who in Hellenistic times translated the Old Testament into Greek in Alexandria, used *homoiôsis,* the same word that Plato had used. To skillful Platonizing Christians this one sentence in the Old Testament was enough to elicit from it the whole Platonic teaching and to claim that the Biblical Creator god was entirely in harmony with the creator of the Platonic Timaios. This verse from Genesis was cited hundreds, perhaps thousands of times, by the Christians, always to the end of adopting Platonic teaching. We can in principle sympathize with these Christian Platonists, and the names of Clement and Origen will always be mentioned with respect and esteem. But after them followed lesser spirits, who used Platonic words in nonsensical contexts with most unpleasant consequences.

When Plato used the term *homoiôsis,* he was thinking of God and Man, and in Genesis the case is the same. This concept is suitable for a connection between two partners. Unfortunately, Christians later tried with the help of this word to define the position of Christ between God and man, and said that the Son was 'essentially similar' *homoiousios* to the father. Other theologians countered that this was false: the Son was 'essentially identical' with the Father, *homoousios.* A concept that had been intended for two partners was applied instead to a triangular situation, and so arose the absurd dogmatic strife over the *iota.* This happened because the theologians were using a concept that was not applicable to the subject treated. When people use words that are really not applicable, then they talk past each other and come to quarrels. They lose the thread of their argument, because the unsuitable word gives no help in providing the precise expression that they seek, and at the end they themselves no longer know what the argument was about. This was the case of the theologians who fought about the *iota.*

It was not the adoption of philosophical concepts that was at fault, but the way these concepts were used. The word *homoiôsis,* to Platonizing philosophers, had been a sort of abbreviation for longer sequences of thoughts about man trying to become similar to god. It was not meant to serve as a rigid definition, but as a kind of motto indicating thoughts which one could also explain fully in detail; the important thing was what was meant and not the single word. If one wants a given thought to remain alive, one must be able to explain it in different fashions changing all the time; what is meant is to be seen from the whole proposition, and the single word also gains its precise significance only in the proposition or in the context of several propositions. What is important is to remain flexible, in words and also in thought. What was wrong, therefore, was the use one made of philosophical words. It was often prescribed that one special word in one definition be used and no other, and this was done within a single system, which was rather closed. In this way words became petrified and were used as if they were permanent objects. They became slogans and were used for quarreling instead of for gaining knowledge. Yet, not the single words are important, but rather the living meaning that is bound up with them.

THE EDITING OF 19TH-CENTURY TEXTS

Morse Peckham

THE EDITING OF 19TH-CENTURY TEXTS

Morse Peckham
(with David R. King)

It is my conviction that the current theory and practice of editing 19th-century texts suffers from a good many illusions. Indeed, I think this general statement applies to the editing of texts from earlier centuries and the 20th as well, although I shall limit myself to the 19th. Several years ago I published a paper, "Reflections on the Foundations of Modern Textual Editing," and it seems proper, since it cannot be expected that very many of my readers will be familiar with it, to present some conclusions, for the present paper is a continuation of the line of argument developed there.

What a textual editor does is to decide that each existing version of a particular work is unsatisfactory and then, with the aid of such evidence as he can accumulate, to construct another version which he claims is more satisfactory. He does not recover the original text as the author intended it; he cannot because those intentions are either irrecoverable or, if surviving, their relevance cannot be demonstrated until the editor has completed his own text. He cannot create a definitive edition; for his efforts rest upon reconstructing an enormously complicated interwoven series of human behaviors, the evidence for which is non-existent, and further, he cannot get all of the documentary evidence, because much of it no longer exists. To this I would now add the point that he cannot even use all the surviving documentary evidence, a matter to which I shall return in detail. Further, the author himself, like the text, is a postulated entity, and coherence of behavior in an author can be no more assumed than coherence of behavior in any human being. Thus, to quote the final sentences of that paper, "There is no one set of instructions which can mediate [the editor's] behavior to the exclusion of all other sets. His activities are multipurposeful; his problem empirical; it cannot be solved *a priori.* His situation is open."

To give an example of a textual problem quite common in 19th-century literature, an author may publish over fifty years as many as seven different versions of a poem. It is known that he himself saw all versions through the press. Which should the editor publish, correcting its errors by the other versions? All have been approved by the author, and at one time he determined each to be the final version. The claims for each are equally strong. Various efforts have been made on theoretical grounds to resolve this question. The first version, it has been said, is closer to the original intention. On the other hand it is by no means uncommon for authors to mature intellectually and artistically, and the claims for the last version are just as strong. I have never come across a claim for the middle versions, but it would not be difficult to construct such claims. The point is that the problem cannot be solved on *a priori* or theoretical grounds. In each case the solution depends on the purposes for which the editor is preparing the text. As an example of the kind of problem that emerges from this situation, it is useful to point out that an author correcting his own work has the same relation to the text that an editor has. The author is editing his own work. Nor can it be assumed that he is an ideal editor. In my own work I have come across instances in which the author no longer understood the syntax of the complex sentence he was reading for purposes of correcting for a new edition. In any case, whatever the decision, a full textual apparatus, whatever version is chosen, should present variant readings, including this kind of error, of all of the other versions. But the presentation of such variants presents a very serious problem, to which I shall return.

At this point, however, and before proceeding further, I think I should indicate that my concern with 19th-century editing is not merely theoretical. For nearly ten years I was a member of the editorial board of the Ohio University edition of the *Complete Works of Robert Browning,* and a contributing editor. The reason for my separation from that edition last September is painful to contemplate and to discuss, but I must mention it, for it has much to do with what I shall present in this paper. Several years ago I became suspicious of the edition, including my own contributions. I had discovered some errors and I set about to prepare a list of errata to be included as appendices to subsequent volumes. I began by investigating, with the aid of all the material used in preparing the edition, the first two volumes. I discovered more than 600 errors before I gave up in utter despondency. I suspect that if I had completed my examination I would have discovered at least 800 and probably more. The errors are found in every category of the edition: the text, the variants, the explanatory notes, and the typographical layout. It was clear to me that the edition was a failure. I recommended that it be abandoned, and resigned. It is, I think, perhaps the worst edition of any serious pretensions that has ever been published, though I am assured that the New York University Press edition of Walt Whitman is, in the words of one eminent textual critic of American authors, "so much waste paper." Further, argument has raged around the editions done under the direction of the Center for the Editions of American Authors (the CEAA), an organization which is part of the Modern Language Association of America and the publications of which are in part supported by grants from the National Endowment for the Humanities. One qualified individual I know asserts that all of the CEAA editions will have to be done over.

From all this one lesson is fairly clear. Only recently has serious editing of 19th-century English and American literary works been undertaken, except for editions of the major Romantic poets, and as work proceeds the problems become more and more serious and baffling. The various volumes of the editions now in progress seem to come out more and more slowly, and very few editors now at work on these editions will live to see their completion. The editing of 19th-century texts has encountered grave difficulties, but the fundamental difficulty is one which this conference has been summoned to consider. It is a linguistic problem, and though what I shall say in the rest of my remarks will take us far away from linguistics, nevertheless, the basic problem is central to our considerations here.

The linguistic problem which, as I see it, is at the root of the problem of textual criticism is that of 'linguistic drift.' What this problem comes down to is the fact that no human being can learn even his native language perfectly. The speech of every individual differs in observable ways from the speech of every other speaker of that language. Even if there is such a phenomenon as deep structure, even if there are linguistic universals, even if they are transmitted genetically—and I cannot myself accept any of these Chomskyan propositions—the learning of a specific language is learning behavior, and the fact that is most interesting for our purposes is that the learning process is not and cannot be completely successful. Chomsky has focussed upon the problem that children, in learning a language, are able to make up sentences which are recognizable as what he calls well-formed sentences but which are not like any sentences they have ever heard. It should of course also be pointed out that they are also capable of making sentences which are not well-formed but to which the response is, judging by their behavior, an appropriate response.

To my mind the notion of the well-formed sentence is a singularly unfruitful one, for it implies that sentences that are not well-formed are deviations or failures. The well-formed sentence notion draws attention away from the equally interesting phenomenon of similar deviations from what are judged to be phonemic and morphemic norms. But as we all know, such norms are constructs, abstractions, categorizations of observable speech phenomena. The well-formed sentence also draws attention away from the phenomenon that speakers of a language are constantly being subjected to direct and indirect instruction about how a well-formed sentence ought to be constructed. And this instruction is not confined to children but is a life-long process. Further, the higher the cultural level to which the individual attains the more direct instruction and correction he receives about well-formed sentences. Editors of publishing houses and journals know perfectly well that even the best authors need correction. One of the most menacing problems of a textual editor is to decide whether a badly-formed sentence which the author has seen in MS, typescript, galley, page-proof, and page is there because the author had observed its malformation and decided to let it stand, or whether he had overlooked it.

That phenomenon which we call overlooking an error is central to the problem of editing and to getting editions through the press. Yet overlooking is the same phenomenon as that responsible for deviations, if we are to call them that, from the well-formed sentence. It is another manifestation of the imperfect learning of one's own language; the only counter-measure in publishing is exhaustive proof-reading. Hyder Rollins is said to have proof-read his editions of Elizabethan poem collections fourteen times. One would think that would be successful, but I know of a volume in the CEAA series which was proof-read fourteen times by six people working in a variety of pair combinations, reading the text aloud. Yet on one page "qircumstance" still stands. In the publishing process, then, are highly visible the two most significant features of linguistic behavior for the textual editor: the individual tendency to deviate from norms, and the social effort to counter that deviation.

However, a norm is not a phenomenally observable entity. At best it is an averaged expectancy; it can be a culturally redundant instruction. As behavioral scientists and linguists use it, it is a verbal construct. Even if we assume that there is such a phenomenon as the well-formed sentence and that it is not a mere constructed norm, it is apparent that we are constantly exposed to and responding appropriately to utterances which are either not sentences or not well-formed sentences. Yet such exposure is by no means the only factor, or even perhaps the most important factor, responsible for the imperfect learning of a language. I am using 'imperfect' ironically, of course, for I wish to call into question the notion of linguistic competence. It seems to me that a child who cries until he gets his bottle is linguistically competent. I do not mean that he has engaged in covert verbal behavior such as, "I want my bottle and I am going to cry until I get it," but merely that when he gets it he stops crying. Now my spoken Italian is quite poor; yet when I am in Italy I get food, lodging, directions, books, transportation tickets—and I get what I want. My respondents are frequently amused and often initially puzzled, but I make it. In certain situations, then, my Italian is competent. On the other hand, when I try to talk with or read physicists my English is frequently incompetent. Moreover, when I read Browning's *Sordello,* there are passages for which my English is incompetent, though I have read it twenty times. When I first read that poem, I was incompetent in English at least half the time. In short, competence is not an objective phenomenon, independent of judgement, but is always a judgement by someone; a judgement of competence is always a normative judgement, not a descriptive one. Anyone who speaks a language is always using it, in someone's judgement, both competently and incompetently.

What this comes down to is that the language that linguists study is a construct, and furthermore a construct in two senses— or at two levels. The linguist himself selects and studies certain features or attributes of linguistic behavior in various combinations, and insofar as he studies those sequences of utterances he calls sentences, he is studying a verbal construct formed by the individual who made the utterance. We like to say that in so doing the individual calls upon the resources of the language. But this is just a metaphor, and not a good one, for it implies that there are resources analogous to the natural resources of raw materials. Of course this is not the case at all. Language is in a continuous state of invention. Perhaps it is not to say very much if one says that the source of the individual's verbal constructions are the verbal constructions he has encountered in the course of his entire life, but it is at least to say something. It is at least to suggest that the statistical possibilities of verbal constructions or utterances are virtually infinite. It is to suggest the possibility that the pursuit of linguistic universals is a futile undertaking. We must never forget that any study of language can be of only a few drops of the vast oceans of language that have been washing about the earth for millions of years, and that the study of language is itself a mode of linguistic behavior, that linguists are using what they purport to be studying.

But this is not the only factor. I have suggested that there are two phenomena of language of particular pertinence to the present problem: the continuous invention of language, that is, the constant and steady phenomenon of linguistic innovation; and the counter-measure of linguistic behavior, the interactional effort to limit that innovation within socially validated linguistic channels. The first let us call the individual factor and the second the interactional factor. One attribute of the individual factor I have already glanced at—the enormous range of linguistic behavior to which any individual is exposed. A far more important attribute is the capacity for randomness in verbal behavior, for behavior that deviates from the learning models the individual has encountered.

The explanation for this latter phenomenon is now readily available. What is true of verbal behavior is true of all behavior, and any general theory of behavior, under which any theory of linguistic behavior must be subsumed, has to account for two phenomena, the individual tendency towards randomness of behavior and the interactional effort to control that randomness and to channel behavior. That effort I call 'policing,' for so far as I can grasp the matter I can see no ultimate sanction for limiting randomness other than the application of physical force. 'Society' is the explanatory word which ultimately subsumes observations of repeated interactional patterns. Thus the ultimate sanction for society is force. There is no choice in the matter, for interaction depends upon predictability of behavior, and predictability of behavior depends upon controlling randomness of response. The source of that randomness is the brain itself, the processes and resultant observable behavior of which are stochastic in character, that is, it produces sequences of events the probabilities of which are constantly changing. We may I think presume that in the course of evolution increasing quantities of behavior came to be transmitted not genetically but by learning. That is, the brain in the course of evolution became increasingly capable of stochastic process. Thus, one definition of stochastic is simply 'randomness.' I think, however, that since random phenomena are capable of being reduced to non-randomness, that is, predictability, by statistical penetration, it might be better to say that the observable behavioral manifestations of the brain's stochastic processes are judged to be random by one whose standard of judgement is a culturally validated and channelled behavioral expectancy. The more that expectancy is violated, the more difficult interaction becomes, including the individual's interaction with himself; since for the purposes of this kind of analysis the individual is most usefully regarded as a social dyad. Culture, which emerges long before man does, may be usefully understood as a counter-adaptation to the judgement of randomness.

From this point of view it is clear enough what the textual editor is engaged in doing. The transmission of a text, insofar as it involves human behavior, necessarily results in a certain amount of randomness of response on the part of the transmitter, provided that the transmitter is human or is a machine made by a human. There is no question, however, that there are now machines capable of transmitting a text with a far lower degree of randomness than can be obtained by a human. The appearance of such machines changes the whole problem, and has been changing it for a long time in ways to which textual editing has by no means adequately responded. The textual editor, then, is engaged in policing what he judges to be the randomness which in fact is inseparable from the process of textual transmission.

The first problem is that it cannot be known whether or not a perfect text has been printed. There may very well be all manner of error-free texts in existence, but whether or not they are error-free cannot be discovered. There are two reasons. First, the transmission of a text—whether it be copied by hand or set up in type and read in galley, proof, and page—necessarily results in a high probability of randomness, that is, departures from the text being copied which someone will judge to be errors. The second reason is that proof-reading a text, no matter what stage it is in, is also a behavioral process, also one that necessarily will contain a certain degree of randomness, and therefore also one which necessarily results in a high probability of random overlooking of errors. Thus a text can be read a hundred times by a hundred different pairs of readers, but certainty of perfection cannot be arrived at. Since that degree of work is never done and really, for economic reasons, cannot be done, one must assume that any text includes errors, though one cannot know where the errors are. For example, one of the most common errors is the omission of 'not' from a sentence. In any number of cases it cannot be determined from the context whether or not the word was in fact omitted, though the meaning of the sentence is utterly changed.

Thus the history of edition-making is a history of repeated efforts to attain perfection; and not so much the repeated failure to do so, but rather the necessarily repeated failure to be certain that perfection has been achieved. Now the scholar needs that certainty. If his argument hinges upon a passage, he needs to be certain that it is free of error, but he cannot be certain. Consequently the cautious scholar never depends upon an edited text if he has at his disposal all the materials, MS, proofs, editions, and so on that should have been used to constitute the text. But to get them is a long and usually costly process. Hence the ideal is to publish a text with all of the variants from all the pertinent materials. But here again the same problem arises. In the complete works of an author whose books went in his lifetime through numerous editions, all of which he supervised, and if MSS and proofs and galleys and author-corrected copies are available, as they often are—and the more recent the author the more often—the variants can amount to millions. The collection, recording, and reproduction of these variants is in itself an enormous task, and of course subject to exactly the necessary intrusion of randomness to which the text itself is subject.

The next problem is even more severe, and one which has in fact scarcely been recognized, except by a very few bibliographical analysts. Actually, I know of only three. The establishment theory of bibliographical analysis is that the history of the printing of a book can be recovered. These few individuals, however, have wondered about that. They have gone to printers and asked them. The answer they receive is raucous laughter. Briefly, the intrusion of randomness in the complex of interacting behaviors involved in printing a book is horrendous. I give but one example. Unbound sheets are stored until they are bound, sometimes for years, for it is not the practice to bind all copies of a book. While they are stored anything can happen. The roof can leak, and a sheet has to be reprinted. When that happens, galleys and page-proofs are not sent to the publisher, let alone to the author. They are not even informed of it. There is no record of it, since, as it is the responsibility of the printing house, no bill is to be submitted to the publisher. This is just one of a thousand possibilities. In short, the establishment theory pays insufficient attention to the human behavior involved in printing, for it is bewitched by what it believes to be a mechanical process, and hence has yet to recognize the immense intrusion of randomness into a process of which the mechanical factor is but a minor element.

The third problem is more severe still, and has, so far as I know, been scarcely recognized, and the implications certainly have not been. One bibliographical analyst has proposed and has given examples of much more detailed and exhaustive quantitative bibliographical analysis than has previously been attempted, only to be attacked by another bibliographical analyst because the results, if these more demanding methods were widely used, would be the proliferation of bibliographical data beyond the point of usefulness. This is, of course, the recognition that the current theory would break down under the weight of increased data. But in fact, it has already broken down, though no one seems to know it. Two factors are at work here, both of which are responsible for such an increase of bibliographic data that the current theory becomes useless.

The fundamental principle of that theory is that it is possible to reconstruct the history of the printing of a book and to discover all the data which need to be taken into consideration so that a definitive edition might be constructed. The theory is thus a historical and genetic theory. Its origins are, of course, in the editing of classical texts from medieval MSS. In such problems each MS presents unique randomness. Furthermore, the materials are reasonably limited. To be sure, the survival of MSS is, like the survival of all historical documents, the consequence of an impenetrably random process. That is, statistics sets out to discover the structure of the distribution of a population, but it cannot proceed without first postulating a theory of that structure. The survival of historical documents is impenetrable to such a theory. Consequently, the discovery of each hitherto unknown classical MS or papyrus fragment is of significance and can result in rather striking changes in the text.

With the onset of printing, however, the situation begins to change. From set type can be produced a series of identical exemplars. The emphasis must be on the 'can be produced,' for in fact one can never be certain that the type itself has not been changed, and one can be reasonably certain that it probably has. That is, the unit of inquiry becomes the type page, and it is changes in that type which result in variants. The effort of the history of printing has been to reduce the randomness necessarily at work in printing from type so that the type cannot change in the course of the printing of the book. This ideal has never been achieved in metal type, or even in plates cast from metal type, though that was a great improvement, introduced in the 19th century. But the problem of the production of identical exemplars is not the only problem, though it is the only problem which current theory has concerned itself with. The quite separate problem is the survival of exemplars. From the earlier centuries of printing relatively few exemplars of most books have survived by, once again, an impenetrably random process. But even from the 17th century some books have survived in embarrassing numbers. Such is the case with the Shakespeare First Folio. There is no doubt that Hinman did a tremendous task when he collated so many exemplars of that book, but the significant point is that he did not collate all existing exemplars. Now, no matter how sophisticated one's statistics may be, all exemplars means all exemplars. No statistical manipulation can make the variants found by examining *some* exemplars equivalent to the variants that might be found by examining *all* existing exemplars; and in the same way, the variants found in all existing exemplars cannot be made equivalent to the variants found in all the exemplars ever printed from those type-pages.

When we get to the 19th century the problem is acute, and by the end of the century it is totally unmanageable. While still involved with the unfortunate Ohio Browning edition, I undertook to locate copies of the 1888-89 and 1889 editions. I sent inquiries to more than 500 libraries in the English-speaking world and with little difficulty located nearly a hundred copies of each. They turn up quite frequently in second-hand and antiquarian booksellers catalogues, both here and in England. Just recently I saw five sets in such a catalogue, and six sets in an antiquarian bookstore. A determined effort could locate hundreds of copies with not too much trouble. Now some of those poems went through four, five, and six re-writings. It would not be difficult to discover several hundred copies of each of them. When it comes to a popular work such as *Huckleberry Finn,* which went through numerous editions, some of which were overseen by the author, the number of copies that might be located would run into the thousands. A 'definitive' edition, as I understand it, in classical MS editing means that all known variants have been considered and recorded. Let us consider, however, current practice.

At this point I must, regretfully, be harsh. The current policy of the CEAA is to collate for each edition of a book five or six copies, with inquiries about special problems, very limited in number. The simple fact is that the probability of discovering all the variants in an edition of 2000 copies, for example, by collating five copies is one to a figure of astronomical size. What this comes down to is that by collating five copies you have discovered the variants in those five copies, but you are not in a position to say anything whatsoever about variants in the remaining 1995. Nor, let me repeat, had you collated 500 surviving copies, would you be in a position to say anything whatsoever about the remaining 1500 exemplars. To repeat, all the variants means all the variants, not just the variants you have taken the trouble to discover. I have asked an important official of the CEAA why collation was so limited, and the answer I received was that that is all that anybody can do. We have here a classical example of the history of science, analogous to the failure of the epicycle theory of planetary motion. A theory is created to handle the data available. The availability of more data than the theory can handle means that the theory collapses. Thus the increased numbers of exemplars printed and the great increase in the numbers of exemplars surviving has so increased the data available that, under the present theory, the increase is simply ignored. The CEAA claims to be producing definitive editions, but it is producing whited sepulchres.

But this is not the only problem. The history of the physical sciences shows, I think, that that history is really the history of scientific instruments. For scientific instruments, invented to make more data available, by so doing undermine the theory responsible for the invention by making available not only more data than the theory can handle, but very frequently kinds of data which the theory had not anticipated. That is, the effect of an innovative instrument is frequently, and most importantly, the randomization of a data population; and I think that the history of statistics shows that statistics becomes more refined as the data it deals with becomes quantitatively greater and increasingly random. That is what has happened in bibliographical analysis and textual editing. Two instruments have been developed and put on the market which enormously facilitate the collation of exemplars—the Hinman Collating Machine and the Lindstrand Comparator—the first very expensive, the second quite inexpensive, though it works just as well and for some people better. Each cuts down enormously the time over the older head-wagging or reading-aloud collations, and greatly increases accuracy, that is, reduces random responses. However, neither eliminates the random. An expert can collate two exemplars of a book by either instrument; and a beginner, using the same instrument, can discover variants which the expert has missed. We have here precisely the same problem that is involved in any kind of proofing. But the principal effect of these instruments is to increase the amount of reliable data beyond the point at which it can be used. They have undoubtedly reduced the time involved in collation and increased the accuracy, but they have undermined the theory.

These two factors, the increase in survival of exemplars and the instrumental increase in availability of data have, then, destroyed the validity of the current historical-genetic theory. The aim of that theory is to discover the relation between editions in order to eliminate some editions of a work and to include others in the creation of a definitive text. But within an edition the problem has ceased to be a historical-genetic problem. It has become a statistical problem. That is, the proliferation of data means that the theory must be changed from an ideal of discovering all the pertinent data to a pragmatic problem of sampling an immense proliferation of data. But there is no point in just random sampling, as we have seen, though that is what is being done. One must have some notion of what can be discovered that is in fact both discoverable and having been discovered can be used. I can see but one possibility, the discovery of a 'concealed impression' or impressions.

The term refers to a general revision of a text for which there is no indication anywhere in the book. That is, corrections were made in standing type or in plates. This can involve the changing of a single letter or the resetting of a line or two or the resetting of a page. Such changes are not isolated but found scattered with some frequency throughout the book. For example, Professor Warner Barnes collated on the Hinman machine eleven copies of a volume of poems by Elizabeth Barrett Browning and found no variants. In the twelfth copy he found variants on every page. He had discovered a concealed impression. Had he followed the CEAA policy and collated but five or six copies, he would never have discovered it. Volumes of poems tend to be blessedly short, but if you have the problem of editing a 500 page novel, twelve collations are scarcely to be thought of.

One cannot know the structure of the distribution of a second and concealed impression except that it will not have been identical with the distribution of the original impression. One cannot know either whether the second was larger or smaller than the first. One can only be sure that the distribution is not random, that is, that there is not an equal probability of picking up exemplars of each impression. One must make a sample of a respectable number of copies, and a certain number of pages in each copy. Using one copy as an anchor copy, one then collates a selection of pages throughout the book with the same pages in other copies. The question is what is the most economical way of doing this that will yield a 90% probability of discovering a concealed impression. I have given Professor David R. King of the Sociology Department of the University of South Carolina the following problem. Given a book of 320 pages printed on ten sheets and bound in ten gatherings of 16 leaves per gathering, and published in an edition of 200 copies, and hypothesizing that there was a concealed impression—what is the most economical way to discover whether or not there was a concealed impression? It turns out that a collation of only 8 pages distributed randomly throughout the book and taken from 22 copies gives a 90% probability of discovering the concealed collation. This is to assume that the variants are fairly frequent and fairly evenly distributed. A collation of 16 pages in 22 copies carries the probability above 90% and of course increases the probability of discovering a fairly sparse revision. To collate 22 pages in 22 copies gives very near certainty that a concealed impression will be discovered. See graphs, pp. 145-6.

The concealed impression having been discovered, it can then be determined which came first, and whether either or both are to be taken into consideration in constructing an edited text, that is, whether or not they are to be used in deciding on emendations. The advantage of this method is that the editor is not in the position of making unjustified claims about completeness or definitiveness, nor will he be embarrassed when it is pointed out that the examination of exemplars he has not collated reveals variants he has not discovered. Since all that can reasonably be discovered within an edition is the presence or absence of concealed impressions, it is to be assumed that such variants will be discovered. Certainly the overwhelming probability is that they are discoverable.

Of course, such a method does not take care of such a contingency as the following, or does so only with the greatest of good luck. It is always possible that most of that concealed impression was destroyed by a warehouse fire, or during shipment, or remaindered and pulped or sold for scrap paper. Then the probability of discovering a concealed impression if the survival is, say, 500 to 10, is obviously remote. But it appears to me that the limitations of analytic bibliography and textual editing must be faced instead of concealed, and that it would be both more graceful and honest of editors to admit to those limitations instead of boasting what a superb and thorough-going job they have done; instead of making unjustified claims.

These are the basic problems of bibliographic analysis and of getting the material ready for the textual critic, particularly as they emerge in the 19th century. Of the problems involved in emending the text I do not propose to speak, except to reassert that every edition presents unique problems which cannot be resolved *a priori* and theoretically. I turn, then, to the problems involved in publishing the edition.

The first of these is the format of the edition itself. The most important editions now being done are those of the CEAA, plus the Fielding edition and a few others. The Browning edition belongs to this group, or, hopefully, belonged. These are supposed to be scholarly editions, created by and for scholars, and with a secondary use as editions with reprint rights leased to commercial publishers. The CEAA editions, at the insistence, as I understand it, of the NEH, are clean-text editions, with no apparatus at the foot of the page, but all of it in the appendices, where, I must say, it is most clumsily and inconveniently arranged. I have said I would be harsh, and I regret it, but it seems to me these CEAA and non-CEAA editions are absurdities.

First, they are supposed to be scholars' editions, but even with subvention they are so expensive that not very many scholars can afford them, particularly young scholars who need them the most. Even more important, they are much too expensive to ask one's graduate students to buy for use in a course, especially if half a dozen texts are to be used. Moreover, they are not only expensive, they have become more expensive, and they will become still more expensive as inflation continues, and still more inaccessible to scholars, for it inevitably happens that in times of inflation academic salaries lag behind other salaries. Already the book-purchasing margin of the academic income has nearly disappeared. Further, as academic resources become increasingly restricted, the funds available for the subvention of these splendid volumes will become increasingly hard to come by. Already several editions, I understand, are seriously threatened, and some have been abandoned without even the first volume having been published, although several volumes were ready for publication.

A second absurdity is the format itself. With one honorable exception, the Dewey edition, they are all tall, handsome, typographically lavish volumes; some of them, such as the Melville, splendid instances of the typographical art, even, in the case of *Mardi,* absurdly so. The model for such editions is obviously the great series of splendid editions of English and American authors brought out in the 19th and 20th centuries by commercial publishers—a kind of publishing which ceased with the onset of the Great Depression of the 1930s. For most of these editions little care was given to the text. They were not made by or for scholars.

They were commercial publications designed for a market of families who for generations, sometimes for many generations, built family libraries, and for their newly rich imitators. That market no longer exists. Hence commercial publishers do not publish such editions, which are economically and culturally out-moded, at least in England and in this country. Yet this complete-ly outmoded style of edition has been taken as the model for the current crop of editions. Moreover, the preparation cost and printing costs of scholars' editions are much greater, since there is such great expense in proof-reading and in the expensive kind of printing required by textual apparatus. It is said that the average cost for preparing a CEAA volume is $27,000, and this figure does not include the costs of the press where it is published nor the manufacturing costs.

A third absurdity is connected with this one. If you pick up a commercial edition the textual rights for which have been leased from the publisher of a CEAA edition, the probability is over-whelming that you will have in your hand what may be the worst edition of that particular book ever published. Commercial publishers do not lease these rights because they are interested in good texts. They are not. They are interested in the exploitable prestige of a CEAA edition. Consequently, with a few exceptions, they devote even less care to proof-reading these texts, aimed as they are for college and university consumption on a large scale, than they do to an ordinary and ephemeral novel, to which, Heaven knows, they pay little enough attention. Some very re-spectable publishers have brought out editions based on leased CEAA editions which are disgraceful, hardly above the level of cheap pornography. Now the way around this was obvious. The best way to control randomness in reprinting is to reprint by photo-offset. One can never completely control the intrusion of randomness, but photo-offset is a far, far better way to control it than is re-composition. However, the format of most of the CEAA editions is too big, too typographically voluptuous, for this kind of economically viable inexpensive reprint. Obviously, all of these editions should have been in the format of the Dewey edition, the dimensions of the standard quality paperback.

The next problem is the preparation of the editions. Much of the work has been directed only in name by the editors listed on the title-page. A great deal of it, in some cases most of it, has been done by graduate students. Now graduate students, generally speaking, have no great interest in working on editions, nor should they have. They have much more important ways to spend their time, except for the very few who are going to spend their lives as textual critics, and at that fewer are going to than think they are. They are interested in supporting themselves, or in pleasing a professor who has control over their careers, or in avoiding teaching, which is much more time-consuming and leaves them less freedom to pursue their proper studies. Moreover, that which is not done by graduate students is done by faculty members many of whom have not even been trained in textual criticism, let alone bibliographical analysis. The Browning edition was not the only one undertaken by people who should not have been doing it.

Of even greater significance is the fact that the typical faculty member is the wrong kind of personality to do either collation or proof-reading, not to speak of the absurdity of a highly-paid professor doing the kind of work which in publishing houses is done by an individual who gets a third of professorial salaries, and is done better. Commercial publishers now have tests which they administer to prospective proof-readers. I know of no case in which either graduate students or faculty members who are working on an edition take such a test. The fact is that most academics are not good proof-readers, for the reason that they have very high expectancies about what they ought to see, and consequently a very high tendency to see it when it is not there. A good proof-reader is a literal-minded individual; but professors have a wide range of responses to any verbal cue. A good proof-reader has no such range and need not even be particularly intelligent. And even then no proof-reader can be perfect. Scholars should have only two things to do with an edition. First, bibliographical analysts should determine what needs to be collated; and after the preliminary collation is done by specially trained proof-readers, should then determine what editions should be used to create the text. Professional proof-readers should collect the variants. With this information the textual critic then makes the emendations. All the rest should then be done by professional proof-readers. And what has to be done by them is an enormous task, for the edition has to be checked numerous times against the variant material (not just the collected variants) at MS, galley, page-proof, and printed sheet stages. The last is essential so that final errata may be included in the front-matter and bound into the book.

All this is an enormous task, it is tremendously expensive, each volume is bound to be costly, and the market must be necessarily small, a factor which drives up the price even higher. And the results cannot be relied upon. Even after all this, the careful scholar will go back, if he can, to the original materials. The most valuable work in the edition will be the work of the bibliographical analyst; but, for reasons I have given above, at the present time even that is of very limited value. All this is exceedingly expensive and time-consuming to do, and it need not be done. There is a simple and inexpensive and rapid and better way of doing it.

First, the problem of collation can be greatly simplified. Since there is no statistical difference between collating five or six copies of an edition and simply using the first one that comes along, the only collation required is between different editions. In most of the CEAA editions that I have examined, there are but one or two that need be considered. The only mildly difficult problem is to discover concealed impressions, and we have seen how easily that is accomplished. In the great majority of cases there is no need to record the variants. All that need be done is to underline the variants from the preceding edition. The textual critic spreads out these marked copies before him and enters in the margin of a xerox copy of the text selected to be emended the emendations required, with a caret to indicate where they go. It is a rare 19th-century edition which has more than two or three emendations per page, and many of them require an emendation only every ten pages or so.

The second stage is to employ an expert calligrapher. In a clean copy of the chosen text he copies in his beautifully readable script the emendations and the carets. That copy is then reproduced by photo-offset. It can be sold at a price any scholar can afford and even require his graduate and undergraduate students to purchase. Because it is photo-offset it will be cheaper than any edition newly composed—far cheaper.

The advantages, I think, are obvious, but are worth dwelling upon. First, the social and economic investment in putting the work of a major author into print is very great. It is wasteful to do it all over again, especially with the necessary result that though errors are removed new errors will be introduced. Second, all of the possibilities of randomness in putting a book through a press are eliminated. There remains only the randomness of photo-offsetting, which has reached a stage of virtual perfection. Third, the discovery of new material, such as unknown but important proof-sheets, or a missing MS, or a hitherto unknown edition put through the press by the author, requires only that a second impression of the calligraphic edition be made, with the new emendations added. Like the first impression, a preface will justify all emendations. It need only be stated on the title-page that it is a second impression and that new emendations have been made. Consequently, the problem which now obtains is avoided. At present, whenever new material is discovered an existing edition is completely outmoded; and that requires, if the traditional way is used, a complete resetting and putting through the publishing process of a new book. But the expense of doing so is so great that frequently years pass by before important textual discoveries become current. The result of a new edition will be a still greater uncertainty about the reliability of the edition, for it must necessarily be assumed that new errors have intruded. What the calligraphic edition offers is the maximum of perfection and reliability with the minimum of labor and cost, as well as unavoidable information about what emendations have been made. It also makes it possible for a scholar to reject an emendation and persuade the original editor to remove it in the next impression. If editions of 19th-century authors are needed (and there is some doubt about that, to tell the truth), we need them now, not thirty years from now, and we can have them now. I would also suggest that the same principle can be applied to earlier texts, including classical texts. Let a group of competent scholars determine the best text of a classical author now available and reissue it calligraphically. Thus texts need not lag years behind the discovery of new material.

There remains the problem of making variants available. The present system of recording variants requires the reconstruction of the line or passage involved. Aside from the fact that there is no standard way of recording variants nor, do I think, can there be, this always presents difficulties. If the material is available, one always turns to the edition with the variant, for, as I have pointed out, variants are not to be trusted. But the problem is resolved very easily. All that is required is that a copy or a first-class xerox of a copy of each variant edition be underlined to indicate the variants from the next previous edition. These variant editions are then reprinted by photo-offset, bound in paper, and packaged in a box. The scholar then has before him all the materials he needs. He need not reconstruct—a matter which often is a little uncertain—for he has the whole reading before him. He can discover variants which have been missed—and there are always such—and he can propose new emendations to be incorporated, if accepted, in the next impression of the calligraphic text. The current way of doing editions creates a closed, a dead-end situation of certain unreliability. The calligraphic text and the variant boxes together create an open situation, capable of almost endless modification with the least possible expense and the highest possible reliability. For example, when a new impression is made of a calligraphic text it is not necessary to re-photograph the entire text but only the page or at most the sheet with the emendation, whichever is the least trouble and expense. A further point is that if the printer is allowed to produce the calligraphic texts in his free time, the cost can be reduced by as much as 20%.

One further advantage is worth mentioning. If a commercial publisher wishes to produce a non-calligraphic edition, one that incorporates the emendations in the text, he need only give the calligraphic text to the printer, striking out the characters for which the marginal emendations are to be substituted. It is up to him to bring out a decent edition. But the scholar and the serious reader are freed of the current dependence upon printers and publishers. To give an example of what all this means: it would be possible to bring out the thirty-four volumes of Browning's works, as originally published, in a calligraphic edition for a total price of less than $100.00, in paper; and it could be done in two years. Further, it would be possible to bring out the variant boxes of nearly 200 MSS, proofs, and editions of his works for around $800.00. For purposes of comparison, the Browning edition, if complete, will probably end by costing around $350.00. Not only is it unreliable, but already the edition of *Sordello* has been outmoded by the discovery of the proofs of the first edition.

To conclude—because of the unavoidable character of linguistic behavior, the history of edition-making shows that reliable editions cannot be created; it shows that the current way of making editions creates a closed or dead-end situation which requires that the effort be repeated, and must again fail. The two-fold accumulation of data for 19th-century and even earlier books which is not assimilable by the current theory has undermined that theory; statistical analysis needs to be introduced into the theory. The current way of making 19th-century editions is in many ways absurd and in any case is technologically outmoded. Textual critics need no longer strive to do what they cannot do; within their grasp is a technology which will result in a greater reliability of editions than they have ever achieved.

Probability of Finding Hidden Impression by No. of Changes per Page and No. of Pages Examined

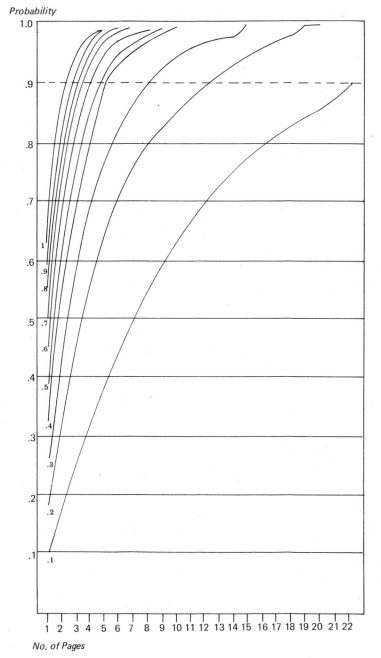

Probability

No. of Pages

145

Probability of Finding Hidden Impression by Sample Size and Printing Distribution

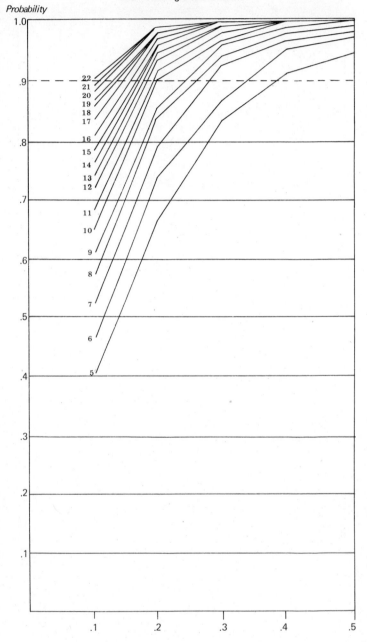

Percentage of total printed copies of concealed impression
n=number of book copies in sample

146

THE ANCIENT IN THE MODERN:
ANCIENT SOURCE MATERIALS IN
PRESENT-DAY HEBREW WRITING

Chaim Rabin

THE ANCIENT IN THE MODERN:
ANCIENT SOURCE MATERIALS IN
PRESENT-DAY HEBREW WRITING

Chaim Rabin

I. *Introduction.*

Modern Hebrew has achieved some celebrity as a revived language. It is therefore necessary to open our discussion with a definition and brief description of its revival. The metaphor expressed by the term 'revival' is apt to be misleading if we take it in the literal sense of bringing something dead back to life, of re-using for communication in a society a language which previously had not served any communicative purposes whatever. To the best of my knowledge, no case of this is on record, though an attempt of this kind is being made at present with the Cornish language and has had a limited measure of success. The various known revivals of languages are rather revivals in the sense in which a tired person is 'revived' by a rest or a drink: a language that has lost some of its uses in a community regains one or more of them; or a language which has ceased to be used by part of a community, but was retained by another part, comes to be used once more by all, or by a significantly larger part of that community.

In the case of Hebrew, the uses that were lost are those pertaining to the spoken language. Probably in the third century A.D., it ceased to be employed amongst any part of the Jewish people as an everyday vehicle of communication. It continued to be used orally as the language of prayer. We also have scattered references throughout the Middle Ages to Hebrew serving as a means of communication between Jews who had no other language in common.[1] A particularly interesting instance of this is Palestine in the late 18th and most of the 19th centuries, where highly conservative religious groups co-existed, each using its home language for inside

[1] Cf. Cecil Roth, *Personalities and Events in Jewish History* (Philadelphia 1953), pp. 136-42.

communication, but employing Hebrew as a lingua franca for trade and for furthering their common interests.[2] In many places, Hebrew was spoken when Jews wished to converse in the presence of outsiders without being understood by them. At times when religious rulings forbade speaking, e.g., between washing the hands for a meal and pronouncing the blessing over the bread, it was considered permissible to speak Hebrew. Some pious men spoke only Hebrew on the Sabbath. Of course all these occasional language uses did not amount to a language of everyday communication, nor was the competence of the speakers anything like that of people speaking their own language. Probably Hebrew was spoken less amongst those who knew it than medieval Latin was spoken among those who had a sufficient knowledge of the latter, even though a fair to good knowledge of Hebrew was much more widespread among Jews than a similar knowledge of Latin among Christians.

The written uses of Hebrew, on the other hand, and the ability to read and understand it, never ceased altogether. Its use was probably at an ebb at the time when it ceased to be spoken. In that period, it seems, only Jews in Palestine and Babylonia (present-day Iraq) could read Hebrew, while amongst others only the letters of the alphabet and a few words were known. From the fourth or fifth century onwards, the written use of Hebrew spread steadily, until by the tenth century all parts of the Jewish diaspora employed it either as the sole written language or side by side with another written language, e.g., in Arabic-speaking countries by the side of Arabic written in Hebrew characters. Literacy being practically universal among Jewish males, and literary activity intensive, Hebrew was used for all purposes for which written languages were used in the Middle Ages: religious writings, philosophy, science and medicine, communal administration, business, private correspondence, diaries, stories, essays, poetry, and even scatology. It proved to have sufficient elasticity to adapt itself to all these uses, and to generate vocabulary and syntax as required. In this it resembles medieval Latin, classicizing Greek, Classical Arabic, and medieval Sanskrit, none of which were by then any longer spoken languages.

---

[2]Cf. T. Parfitt, "The Use of Hebrew in Palestine 1800-1882," *Journal of Semitic Studies* 17 (1972) 237-52.

Like Latin, towards the end of the Middle Ages Hebrew began to recede in its written uses before the spoken languages of its users. A number of specific Jewish languages began to enter popular literature and even devotional writings: Yiddish, Judaeo-German,[3] Judaeo-Spanish, Judaeo-Arabic, Judaeo-Persian, Judaeo-Italian, Judaeo-Berber, and others. In the nineteenth century there arose also specific Jewish literatures in standard German, French, English, Russian, Arabic, etc. Correspondingly the percentage of those possessing a writing and reading competence in Hebrew rapidly diminished. This process was much slower in Eastern Europe, as well as in North Africa and the Middle East. A modern, European-style Hebrew literature started in Germany, Holland, and Italy in the 18th century, and in the 19th century developed in Eastern Europe into a literature of considerable force, though its circle of readers remained limited. One of the results was that people who had broken away from traditional Hebrew religious education did not necessarily pass to other languages, but at least in part joined the ranks of those who read and wrote the new-style secular Hebrew. The latter was distinguished from the traditional style by strict classicism in the Biblical manner. Thus by 1880, Hebrew, while the number of its speakers was receding, was still vigorous as a written language.

The re-introduction of Hebrew as a spoken language in everyday conversation, in the family, and in school teaching as a medium of instruction, in other words as a normal language of communication, was urged by Russian-born Eliezer Ben-Yehuda (1858-1922), first in an article written in France and published in Vienna in spring 1878, and subsequently in Palestine by personal example and influence and in newspapers edited by him.[4] When his first son was born in 1882, he insisted on bringing him up entirely in Hebrew. The movement initiated by Ben-Yehuda and his friends—in the face of almost unanimous rejection by the Hebrew literary and scholarly establishment—was strengthened by

---

[3]The addition "Judaeo-" to the name of a language refers in principle to the use of Hebrew letters for writing it and of Hebrew words for religious and related ideas. However, in almost all cases there are additional differences between the general and the Jewish forms of such languages.

[4]For a sociolinguistically oriented history of the revival, cf. Jack Fellman, *The Revival of a Classical Tongue* (Hague 1973); id., "The Role of Eliezer Ben-Yehuda in the Revival of the Hebrew Language," in J. A. Fishman, ed., *Advances in Language Planning* (Hague 1974), pp. 427-55.

young people who emigrated to Palestine from the Russian empire after the pogroms of 1881 and under the continuing anti-Semitic pressure there, and settled in Jaffa and in newly-founded agricultural settlements. By 1890 a number of Hebrew-speaking schools were functioning, and in 1914 pupils and teachers throughout the country revolted against the plan to diminish the role of Hebrew in high schools,[5] thus providing the emergence of a nationalist attitude towards their spoken language. In 1916, 34,000 persons declared in a census that Hebrew was their language of daily communication.

There are indications that the spoken language soon began to develop linguistic features which set it apart from the written styles used at various periods since 1880. At first these were ignored or treated as learners' mistakes, an attitude which has by no means lapsed even now.[6] Some awareness of the permanency of these divergencies began to appear in the 1930s, when they were described by teachers, in scholarly journals and in books, as faults in the language of children. About the same time the colloquial occasionally made its appearance in dialogue in fiction, mainly to characterize children or uneducated people. During and after the 1948 War of Independence, young local-born writers adopted a narrative style deeply influenced by the colloquial. However, this movement ceased abruptly, and its foremost exponents changed to accepted literary standards. In 1955 the first pieces of linguistic research on the colloquial language were published,[7] and soon such research became academically respectable. In the 1960s, features of the colloquial came to be used in dialogue in fiction and drama in the way this is done in Western literatures.

The Classical period of Modern Hebrew literature, however, occurred before the time when colloquial speech gained this limited recognition. Moreover, until the 1920s most Hebrew writers lived outside Palestine. Being in need of a colloquial register for

[5] By establishing a technical high-school in which the subjects such as mathematics and natural sciences were to be taught in German.

[6] Cf. Abba Bendavid, *Leshon miqra u-leshon hakhamim,* I (Tel Aviv 1967), in a chapter entitled "Has Israeli Hebrew Standards?" (pp. 303-29), and especially the section headed "Is there any purpose in scientific description of the language of a society which is in the process of learning it?" (pp. 315-6).

[7] Cf. *Current Trends in Linguistics* VI (Hague 1970), pp. 331-3.

their literary purposes, they developed a 'colloquial' of their own, far removed from the tendencies of the spoken language in Palestine.

In the religious source literature, the Hebrew language appears in two rather distinct forms. The first is Biblical Hebrew, spoken from the 12th to the 6th century B.C.; the second, Mishnaic[8] Hebrew, spoken probably from the 5th century B.C. to the 3rd century A.D. An additional set of religious sources is in Aramaic,[9] the most important being the Babylonian Talmud and the Palestinian Talmud (3rd to 6th cent. A.D.); Mishnaic Hebrew also contains many Aramaic words. In the Middle Ages both forms of Hebrew were used. On the whole Biblical Hebrew was employed for poetry and artistic prose, and Mishnaic Hebrew— with many medieval accretions—for everything else.

Soon after its inception, modern Hebrew literature of the 18th and 19th century rejected Mishnaic Hebrew altogether and used Biblical Hebrew for narrative and scientific prose, and later also for newspapers. For ideological reasons, Mishnah and Talmud were objected to, as being one of the causes of Jewish social and economic backwardness. Yiddish, the spoken language of Eastern European Jews, was also proscribed by the modernists as being another cause of the same. Yiddish happens to have borrowed many words from Mishnaic Hebrew and from Talmudic Aramaic. Therefore Abraham Mapu (1808-67), in his Hebrew novel *The Hypocrite,* published 1857-64, could characterize the speech of the orthodox enemies of Enlightenment by making them use some Mishnaic and Aramaic words, as opposed to the pure Hebrew of his modern, westernized characters, thus suggesting to the reader that the former spoke Yiddish, while the latter presumably spoke German (as many Jewish Enlightened people did) or Russian. S. J. Abramovich (c. 1836-1917), better known under his *nom de plume* Mendele Mokher Sefarim, wrote a realistic novel in 1862 where all characters spoke pure (or almost pure) Biblical Hebrew; but in the course of writing it he came to feel that representing the

[8] So called after the *Mishnah,* an authoritative collection of religious law, compiled about 200 A.D. For the controversy as to whether Mishnaic Hebrew was actually spoken, see *Current Trends,* ibid., pp. 317-9.

[9] Aramaic resembles Hebrew to about the extent that German resembles English. It became an international language during the Persian Empire (539-331 B.C.) and subsequently displaced Hebrew and other Near Eastern languages in spoken use.

Jews of the Russian Pale of Settlement as speaking in sonorous Biblical phrases was contrary to the principles of artistic realism. He turned to writing in Yiddish and became the first major modern author in that language. Twenty-two years later, in 1884, he took up writing Hebrew again, but in a completely new style, in which Mishnaic elements were freely mingled with Biblical ones. The immediate success of this innovation, and its imitation by all his contemporaries, suggests that this admixture of Mishnaic Hebrew was felt to be a literary equivalent of Yiddish. We have indirect evidence for this. In 1904, J. Berkovitz (1885-1967) began to translate into Hebrew the works of Sholem Aleikhem (S. Rabinovich, 1859-1916), whose son-in-law he later became. In his attempt to render the juicy Yiddish of that author, Berkovitz further enriched the mixed Hebrew established by Mendele with words and phrases from the Aramaic of the Babylonian Talmud. The poet C. N. Bialik once referred to this procedure by saying that Berkovitz had Yiddishized Hebrew.[10] Berkovitz's style was, and still is, employed by those who translated Russian fiction into Hebrew, so as to reproduce the colloquial tone of Russian literature. It was still used in the 1960s by Hebrew writers who imitated Yiddish and Russian genres, especially in the picaresque novels fashionable at that time. The idea of using Aramaic—the language of higher religious learning—to form a colloquial register in Hebrew was defended by pointing to the role Aramaic had played in its time as a vernacular vis-à-vis Hebrew—just like Yiddish. . . .

Modern literary Hebrew thus derives entirely from the written tradition of the times preceding the revival of the spoken language, and until quite recently any influence of the revived spoken Hebrew was slight and contrary to the intentions of its writers, in the nature of the interference of a dialect in the use of a standard language. To this there is one apparent exception. The revival of Hebrew in everyday communication necessitated a great deal of vocabulary expansion, whether by forming new words, by borrowings, or by giving new meanings to existing words taken from the old literary sources. These new words do of course appear in modern Hebrew literature, but since vocabulary

---

[10]This is part of an aphorism, the second part of which can be understood either to mean 'and hebraized Yiddish' or 'made Yehudit (his wife) pregnant' (B. *yihed et ha-^{c}ivrit ve-^{c}ibber et ha-yehudit*).

expansion is a feature of Hebrew throughout its history as a purely written language, this use of new words connected with the revival cannot be treated as a change in the character of the written language. It is not even a change in the character of the accretions: medieval and early modern rabbinic writings dealt with matters of everyday life and had to create expressions for innovations in dress, food, economic practices, and mechanical appliances. For instance the modern words for 'brandy' and 'potato' were created long before the revival. Similarly the modernist writers of the 18th and 19th centuries created words for contemporary objects and concepts. Moreover, only a small proportion of the new words since 1880 were created by the man in the street; most were made up either by the 'Language Council'[11] or by other semi-professional guardians of the language, or were in fact created by novelists, essayists, or poets.

Quite a few authors, however, chose to ignore some or all of the new words that had become current in the colloquial, and to replace them by creations of their own or by archaisms, or just to go on using the foreign words. The foremost example of this was S. Y. Agnon.

II. *The 'Sources' and the Modern Language.*

The use of Hebrew in writing only was a case of diglossia, the employment of two distinct languages by one community for different, socially defined purposes.[12] We can distinguish two types of diglossia: one in which the 'upper' language is the living language of some other group, whom it serves as a sole non-diglossic vehicle of communication; and another, where the upper language is a 'classical' idiom no longer spoken anywhere. The very concept of diglossia implies that the upper language is learnt as a second language, and that there must needs be some school system or other educational framework where it is taught, and people whose task it is to transmit it. It is therefore natural that the community has a normative attitude to it, since language learning implies

[11]The Language Council was active in 1880 and in 1904-53, when it was replaced by the Language Academy. Cf. J. Fellman, *International Journal of the Sociology of Language* 1 (1974) 95-103; M. Medan, *Ariel* (Jerusalem), Number 21, 1970.

[12]Cf. C. A. Ferguson, "Diglossia," *Word* 15 (1959) 325-40.

normativity. The model for the norms thus comes from outside the community.

In the first case, that of a living upper language, this model will tend to be the usage of the country or ethnic group where that language is at home. This is still true in those instances where the diglossic community has decided to develop standards of its own in the use of its upper language, for such standards are negations of features of the outside model, yet still use it as a point of reference. The connection with what is naturally seen to be a vehicle of higher cultural values—and will often be a language of wider applicability and usefulness—will be appreciated by the diglossic user community. In its methods of teaching the upper language, such a community will tend to present the learner with texts produced by the 'giver' community, and thus its children will absorb through their school texts the stylistic ideas of another society. A tension is thereby set up between the way in which the member of the diglossic community handles his spoken mother-tongue and the way in which he is taught to handle his cultural language.

What I have called 'handling a language' corresponds to some extent to the idea of 'pragmatics,' but I think has a wider sense. It would include such rhetorical devices as using a restricted or a 'rich' vocabulary, parataxis or hypotaxis, employing adjectives or adverbs lavishly or sparingly, being down-to-earth or rhetorical, the use of metaphor, emphasis, sentence-connectors, 'clarté' or fuzziness and understatement, balancing of sentences, repetitions or stylistic variation, and other features of the sentence, the paragraph, and the complete utterance, such as openings, climax, inner balance, or perorations. These features are quite distinct from the grammar, syntax, and vocabulary of the language. Different nations may use the same structure and dictionary, but handle them in markedly different ways, as for instance English is used in Britain and America. Whenever there is a break in literary continuity, e.g., between Classicism and Romanticism, this will express itself also in the way of handling the literary language. Handling, no less than structure and vocabulary, determines the 'way of thinking' and the 'personality' of the language user. There is evidence that diglossic communities are aware of having such a double personality. Paraguayans told researchers that in Guaraní (the universal spoken language) one can express one's emotions much better than in Spanish, that one can make jokes, that it offers more opportunities for play on words, and that it has shades of meaning lacking in Spanish.[13] It is evident that all these shortcomings of Spanish exist only for speakers of Guaraní, and that the natural speaker of Spanish does not feel hampered in those respects. Anyone close to Yiddish is well aware of a similar attitude with regard to this language. The Hebrew poet C. N. Bialik is credited with the statement 'Hebrew one talks, but Yiddish talks itself.' Goethe, for whom his spoken Frankfurt dialect and literary Hochdeutsch were still a diglossia situation, expressed this in a generalized way:[14]

"Weil dir ein Vers gelingt in einer gebildeten Sprache
die für dich dichtet und denkt, glaubst du schon, Dichter zu sein."

Similarly it has always been the custom in teaching classical upper languages to present the learner with texts from the period when that language was still alive, i.e., spoken, or at any rate is currently believed by the user community to have been spoken. In some cases this is narrowed down to texts from a period when that language is believed to have been at its purest and best, such as Attic Greek for the Roman pupil or Golden Latinity for the medieval learner. In this type of diglossia, however, the very texts of the classical language have an aura of educational values. Often they are basic religious texts, and acquisition of the language and of the religious truths contained in them goes hand in hand. But even if they represent a religion different from that of the learner— as did Latin or pre-Islamic Arabic poetry—the classical texts are supposed to teach societal values, to form the pupil's appreciation of beauty, and to transmit to him suitable modes of expression and thought. Knowing these texts thus constitutes in itself a major social asset. Such knowledge is shown by freely quoting from them. It is a form of social flattery to expect one's conversation partner or reader to identify quotations even if they are not

---

[13]Cf. P. L. Garvin and M. Mathiot, "The Urbanization of the Guaraní Language," in Anthony F. Wallace, ed., *Men and Cultures, Selected Papers of the Fifth International Congress of Anthropological and Ethnological Sciences 1956* (Philadelphia 1960), pp. 783-90. The reference is to p. 788.

[14]From *Xenien;* in English: "Didst thou succeed with a verse in a language worked out and consummate/shaping your thoughts and your rhymes, don't think a poet art thou," P. Carus tr. and sel., *Goethe and Schiller's Xenions* (Chicago 1896), p. 51.

given in full, but only by allusion. In any case, the writers of antiquity are assumed to have expressed ideas in ways so perfect that they cannot be bettered, and therefore it is best to assimilate these perfect formulations by quotation.

In many subtle ways, a classical upper language in diglossia is not a language like any other. Competence in it becomes a function of memory rather than of internalization of structure or transformations. The esthetic uses of language become an ability not merely of using possibilities hidden in its structures and words, but of using possibilities hidden in its texts. One's personal style is achieved by adopting the style of one's favorite classical author, which, in a situation where mental tools for analyzing style are largely lacking, means in fact borrowing his phrases. The ultimate height of this is the 'mosaic style,' in which minute fragments of the ancient texts are combined into new wholes. Great intellectual and esthetic satisfaction may be achieved by the new facets the wording of those fragments reveals in this procedure, and by the 'resonance' of the original contexts for the reader able to identify them, thus adding unsuspected dimensions to meaning.

We shall illustrate this with some examples from different periods. The first comes from the 12th-century Spanish Hebrew poet Jehudah ha-Levi (Hebrew text 1). In a poem for Passover, he makes use of the scene in Judges 5:28, after the death of Sisera: "Through the window she looked forth and wailed, the mother of Sisera, through the lattice: 'Why is his chariotry so long in coming, why do the hoofbeats of his chariots tarry?' "[15] This verse is reinterpreted by Jehudah ha-Levi as Israel's ionging for the Messiah:

"On the day when My prophets shall proclaim to you . . . :
'Though the hoofbeats of My chariots have tarried and been
     kept back,
Yet My mercy towards you has been stirred and has grown
     strong.' "[16]

The reader knew, of course, that the wicked Sisera was dead and his mother's hope not to be fulfilled. The quotation thus stresses

---

[15] Bible quotations are adapted from the Revised Standard Version.

[16] H. Brody, ed., *Diwan des Abu-l-Hasan Jehuda ha-Levi,* III (Berlin 1910), p. 18 = ed. J. Zmora (Tel Aviv 1955-56), p. 210.

that in contrast to the vain hopes of the godless, the expectations of the believer, though delayed, shall be fulfilled, and he was reminded of the words in verse 31, ibid. "So perish all Thine enemies, O Lord; but they that love Him be like the sun as it rises in its might."

Our second quotation comes from a private letter written in the 17th century in Central Europe. The writer composed his missive on a Friday, when all work must cease about an hour before sundown and the Jewish householder is expected to be busy with preparations for the Sabbath. He excuses himself for not writing at greater length, *min duhqā de-kallā*. The words are in Aramaic, and refer in their original context to the crowding (*duhqā*) of people at the periodic popular study assemblies (*kallā*) in the Babylonian Talmudic Academies in the early middle ages.[17] However, both in Aramaic and Hebrew, the verb *dahaq,* from which *duhqā* is derived, means also 'to urge someone on' or 'to be urgent,' thus referring to lack of time rather than lack of space. As for *kallā,* this resembles the Hebrew word *kallah* 'bride.'[18] The Talmud already refers to the Sabbath as the bride of the Jew, and this is brought home to every Jew by the beautiful hymn "Go forth, my friend, to meet the bride" recited as part of the Friday evening prayers. The reader who was sufficiently expert in the Talmud and ingenious enough would thus be able to interpret the Aramaic 'pressure of the assembly' as a 'Hebrew'-Aramaic phrase meaning 'the urgency of the bride.' It was thus an agreeable way to state a trite idea in a striking manner while at the same time establishing the learned status of both writer and recipient of the letter.

This way of using the ancient sources seems to be more developed in Hebrew than in other classical languages, perhaps because the Jewish religion demanded universal male literacy and built the regular study of the principal ancient religious texts into the round of basic religious duties.[19] As far as I am aware, Hebrew

[17] Babylonian Talmud, tractate Berakhoth fol. 6a, where the crowding is said to be caused by evil spirits.

[18] The Talmudic dictionary of Jacob Levy (Leipzig 1876-89) claims that Aramaic *kallā* is the word for 'bride' used in a metaphorical sense, but more probably it is a different word, meaning 'totality' (thus also A. Even-Shoshan, *Ha-millon he-hadash,* III (Jerusalem 1966), p. 1056, s.v. *kallah* 2).

[19] Cf. C. Rabin, "Liturgy and Language in Judaism," in: *Language in Religious Practice,* ed. William J. Samarin (in press).

is the only language to have a special term for it: *melitza*
(mĕlīṣah),[20] and I shall refer to it by that name in our discussion.
It differs from learned allusion by involving a change in meaning,
and often also in form, and differs from play on words or rhetorical figures by having as its raw material a recognizable quotation.
If the reader does not recognize the quotation, or the shift has
become so hackneyed that the quotation is no longer noticed,
there is no melitza.[21]

Beginnings of melitza are found in the Dead Sea Scrolls. It is
in full flower in the Piyyut hymnology (ca. 5th to 10th cent. A.D.)
and is one of the stylistic foundations of medieval Hebrew poetry
in Arabic meters, which started in Spain in the 10th century and
went on into the 18th cent. in Europe and the Middle East. In all
these, its textual basis is the Biblical text exclusively, although it
must be pointed out to the modern reader that the use made of
Biblical verses frequently involves the interpretations of the sacred
text found in Midrash literature (ca. 2nd to 11th cent.) and in
medieval Jewish commentaries. Melitza was equally a feature of
artistic prose, historical works, prefaces of books, and communal
and private letter writing; and from the 16th cent. onwards, when
Hebrew literature began to become more variegated, intruded also
into new types of writing. In prose it increasingly came to include
besides the Bible also quotations from Mishnah, Talmud, Midrash,
and the Aramaic mystical work *Zohar* (13th cent.). Not only are
Biblical and Mishnaic Hebrew not distinguished in this activity,
but as we have seen, Hebrew and Aramaic can also be used to substitute for each other in melitza re-interpretations. The habit of
melitza played a not inconsiderable role in welding together the
various languages of the traditional educational curriculum into a
new functional prose language,[22] and is exhibited in its most
impressive form in the earlier literature of Hassidism (18th-19th

---

[20] A Biblical word (Habakkuk 2:6; Proverbs 1:6), translated by the Revised
Standard Version as 'scoffing' and 'figure,' by the New English Bible as 'insults' and
'parables.' In both passages it has next to it *mashal* 'parable.'

[21] E.g., Modern Hebrew "they came to the Valley of Shaveh" (Genesis 14:17) in
the sense "they arrived at a compromise" (because *shaveh* is 'equal').

[22] Which shows also signs of structural reorganization, and hardly deserves the
harsh judgment of the great Gotthelf Bergstrasser, *Einführung in die semitischen
Sprachen* (Munchen 1928), p. 47: "Mittelalterliches Hebräisch gehort zu den ver-
wahrlosesten Sprachen."

cent.). At the same time it kept alive the consciousness of connection with the Sources by directing the reader's attention to the Source-contexts necessary for the appreciation of the meaning of phrases in contemporary writing.

The biblicizing classicism of early modern Enlightenment (*Haskalah*) literature in the 18th to 19th centuries inhibited the further development of the integrated prose language by depriving it of artistic outlets and reducing it to a technical language of orthodox rabbinic circles. The Biblical prose style which Haskalah introduced, however, did not renounce the use of melitza. It employed it not only as a stylistic device, but also as a means for expressing modern concepts in a language more than two thousand years old. The Haskalah writer was able to rely on his audience knowing the Hebrew Bible thoroughly because of the new attitude to the Bible which characterized his readership. Orthodox Judaism of that age discouraged reading parts of the Bible which were not included in liturgy, and the traditional Jew knew material from outside the Pentateuch, the Psalms, the Five Scrolls, and the weekly Prophetic readings, only through quotations of it in Talmud and Midrash. Reading the whole Bible as a connected text stamped a person as a follower of Haskalah. By expecting him to get the point of Biblical melitza, the Haskalah writer not only flattered the erudition of his reader, but also acknowledged his status as a progressive and enlightened person.

When Mendele Mokher Sefarim created a new integrated Biblical-Mishnaic style in the 1880s, he continued using Biblical melitza, but did not to any marked extent re-introduce Talmudic melitza. Research undertaken at Jerusalem by the late Prof. Y. Kutscher and his students showed that Mendele's Talmudic language material was mainly borrowed from a few tractates of the Babylonian Talmud that were most frequently studied by the common man in Eastern Europe. In other words, Mendele, who was a perceptive observer and critic of his society, was aware that the social basis of the effective use of Talmudic melitza had been weakened, and potential readers could not be relied upon to recognize allusions. The same applies to Chaim Nachman Bialik (1873-1934), whose first poem appeared in 1892, and much of whose poetry was an elegy on the passing of traditional Jewish educational patterns. His use of Talmudic vocabulary is rich, but requires only a recognition of words and idioms, not of original contexts. His use of Biblical material, on the other hand, demands from the reader quite a degree of textual expertise, as may be illustrated by the following quotation from his poem *Ha-Matmid* (cf. Hebrew text 2), where we have underlined the melitza fragments:

"The swallow stirs up its nest, its tender fledglings,
To repeat the praise of the generous light of the sun,
The triumphs of its open-handedness towards the dwellers of
    darkness."

This is put together from the following verses: Deuteronomy 32:11: "Like an eagle that stirs up its nest, that flutters over its young." Judges 5:11: "There they repeat the triumphs of the Lord, the triumphs of His peasantry in Israel." For *pirzono* "His peasantry"[23] Bialik substitutes *pizrono* "his open-handedness" in good melitza tradition. Psalm 143:3: "He has made me dwell in darkness like the eternally dead."

It will be seen that recall of the unquoted end part of Deuteronomy 32:11 is useful in making the link with the 'young' of the poem, though the words are different. The full significance of the use of Psalm 143:3 will be appreciated only by those who recall the unquoted part of that verse. According to Bialik's description of the Yeshiva students, with whose life the poem deals, the words 'dwellers of darkness' are no doubt meant to apply to them, since in later verses they are described as 'eternally dead,' whose youth "is lost forever, like a shadow, as if it was not life."

On the other hand, Eliezer Ben-Yehuda eschewed the use of melitza. Though to the best of my knowledge he did not discuss this matter anywhere, it is safe to assume that this was part of his new attitude to Hebrew as a living, purely functional language. This feature of living Hebrew is thrown into relief by an incident in the life of 'the first Hebrew child,' Ben-Yehuda's son, later known as Itamar Ben-Avi. In 1902 he entered a story of his for a competition arranged by a committee in Odessa. The judges liked his story, but felt they could not award him the prize because he did not use 'expressions' but only 'words,' i.e., because the element of melitza was lacking.

---

[23]The meaning is disputed.

It was one of the Odessa enthusiasts for spoken Hebrew, Joseph Klausner (1874-1958), later to become the first professor of Modern Hebrew Literature at the Hebrew University of Jerusalem, who in 1896 opened the ideological struggle against melitza in an article entitled *Ivrit hadashah,* which can be translated either as "A new Hebrew" or as "Modern Hebrew."[24] He rejects expressions such as "(the son) that came forth from his loins" (1 Kings 8:19), "and he girt up his loins" (ib. 18:46), "the wife of his bosom" (Deuteronomy 28:54),[25] because they are "peculiar and unnatural for any reader in our time" and it would be impossible to translate them exactly into any foreign language. Later on Klausner advocated rejecting all words and grammatical forms found only in the Bible, and urged that Modern Hebrew should link itself to the final stage at which the language had been spoken, viz. Mishnaic Hebrew (spoken ca. 5th cent. B.C. to 2nd cent. A.D.).[26]

The view of Biblical Hebrew and Mishnaic Hebrew as linguistic systems, rather than as collections of exempla for direct imitation, dominates the language-planning studies of Prof. Zeev Ben-Hayyim and Abba Bendavid,[27] who discuss the problems inherent in the integration of these two different systems into one. This is also the attitude of the prescriptive normativists of recent years, who are agreed that it is necessary to abstract from the classical texts consistent structural and semantic rules, and to disregard any deviations from these rules that may occur in the classical Source texts themselves; otherwise "any mistake made to-day can be proved right from the Bible." One of the few things on which Hebrew language teachers in schools agree with their pupils is the rejection of melitza. The last refuge of melitza is in works

[24] Republished in his collected works, volume *Ha-^{c}ivrit ha-ḥadasha u-va^{c}ayoteha* (Tel Aviv 1957), pp. 25-35. The reference is to p. 29.

[25] The renderings here are from the King James Version. The Revised Standard Version replaces the first, but keeps the two others; the New English Bible replaces the first two and keeps the third.

[26] Especially in a brochure "A Living Language or a Pile of Exempla?" (Jerusalem 1935) (reprinted in op. cit. n. 24, pp. 72-8). He wrote a Hebrew grammar along those lines (*Diqduq qaṣar,* etc., 1933-4), and translated the Book of Amos into his Mishnaic-Modern Hebrew (*Sefer ^{c}Amos ^{c}im parshegen,* Tel Aviv 1942-3).

[27] Ben-Hayyim, "Lashon ^{c}atiqah bi-mesi'ut hadashah" ("An ancient language in a new reality"), *Leshonenu La-^{c}Am,* issue no. 35/37 (1952-3). For Bendavid, see note 6.

purporting to teach idioms, most of which insist more on the knowledge of the exact source passage and the context meaning there than on telling their readers what the idioms mean today. The Israeli school-child, who has learnt Hebrew as a first language from his family and his surroundings, and is no longer dependent on classical literature for his basic contact with it, does not read these works at the level of literal attention which enables him to take delight in the subtleties of recall.

III. *Reactivation.*

The preceding remarks on the demise of melitza may appear strange to those who are acquainted with the works of Shmuel Yosef Agnon (1888-1970) and with some of the literature on him. Agnon did not write Modern Hebrew of the literary sort, but a language based entirely upon Talmud and Midrash, with some Biblical influence. His writings read like a mosaic of phrases culled from those sources. Older people, with roots in pre-revival Hebrew literature, enjoy his style as Talmudic melitza.

Characterizations of the meaning of Agnon's stories vary widely, from those who see them as a nostalgic evocation of a traditional simplicity as yet untroubled by the stresses of our modern age, to those who discover in them the demonic tendencies hidden underneath tradition or the horrors of a rootless world. His language, likewise, can be viewed from different angles. On the surface it is naive and artless, but on closer reading it reveals depths of meaning due in part to a concentration of stylistic devices found also in other writers, but to a not inconsiderable measure connected with his use of the ancient Sources.

Prof. Arnold Band has pointed out that at first Agnon experimented with different styles, and used his characteristic language for the first time in the short story ᶜ*Agunot* ("Deserted Women"), published in 1908 (cf. Hebrew text 4). Band claims that it was the success of that story which made him adopt the style for good.[28] Agnon used this style also in ordinary conversation. The Hebrew name which he adopted is formed from the root of the word

---

[28] A. Band, *Nostalgia and Nightmare* (Los Angeles 1968), pp. 57-63; previously in the daily *Ha'aretz* of July 26, 1963.

*c**agunot (^cGN),* an indication of the place this story held in the history of his literary personality. We have therefore chosen an extract from it, in the form in which it was printed as a paperback in 1921,[29] to illustrate the relation between purely linguistic material taken from the classical Sources and identifiable quotations from them, by italicizing the quotations in our translation.

The story tells of the strange attraction of the daughter of a rich Jerusalemite for the young craftsman who built the Ark of the Law for the synagogue which was to be part of the Talmudic Academy the father-in-law set up for his learned future son-in-law. She hears the craftsman, Ben-Uri, singing at his work (cf. Hebrew text 3).

"Dinah, the daughter of Rabbi Achiezer, heard it, at the *window* she placed herself, Dinah the most beautiful. *Through the lattice she looked forth* and inclined her ear to listen, and her heart was drawn to the workshop as if by sorcery, God forbid.

"Dinah went down to see the craftsman's labors, she and her maidservants with her. She looked at the ark, she stirred the tinctures, examined the mouldings, and held the tools in her hand, while Ben-Uri was going about his work, planing down a piece of the Ark as he sang. Dinah heard his voice, *and she did not know her soul. He, too, was directing his voice,* so as to draw her heart with his singing, that she might stand there and not move away for all eternity. Their hearts felt pleasure and fright. *It was hard for them to part.*

"However, as Ben-Uri continued to busy himself with his work, he became much attached to his task. His eyes and heart were absorbed by the Holy Ark, *non est locus vacuus ab eo.* And Ben-Uri *did not think of* Dinah, *and he forgot her.*"

The above translation is meant to be literal rather than literary, and to give some idea of the mixture of Biblical language (rendered in more archaic words) and Mishnaic Hebrew (rendered in ordinary English). For this reason also the Aramaic phrase is

[29] Berlin (Jüdischer Verlag), pp. 10-11. The original version, from *Ha-^comer* 2.1 (1908-9) 53-65, is also reproduced here. It lacks several of the features we discuss, so that it is clear they were put in as a result of developments in Agnon's stylistic thinking. We also reproduce the passage as it appears in the *Collected Stories* (Jerusalem 1953), II, p. 407.

rendered in Latin. Thus I have tried to reproduce what an Israeli reader might feel in reading the passage. Its most outstanding features, however, are the passages from the Sources, which we shall now discuss:

"window . . . Through the lattice she looked forth" is a quotation from Judges 5:28: "Through the window she looked forth and wailed, the mother of Sisera, through the lattice: 'Why is his chariotry so slow in coming, why do the hoofbeats of his chariots tarry?' " The items are somewhat rearranged, and the verb for 'to look forth' is in a different voice. Except for the general atmosphere of anxious expectation (though in entirely different circumstances), there is nothing to connect the context of the Biblical source with that of our passage. However, a link can be established between the two through the re-interpretation by Jehudah ha-Levi which we have quoted (see p. 9 above, and note 16). It is not impossible that Agnon could have seen the poem of ha-Levi even before publication, since both he and its editor lived in the same part of Eastern Galicia. It might thus have inspired him, consciously or unconsciously. But it is most improbable that any of Agnon's readers would have caught this connection.[30]

"She did not know her soul" is based on Canticles 6:12, "I did not know my soul," in a difficult context. The phrase was often used in early modern Hebrew literature. The underlying interpretation runs counter to that by the best-known commentator, Rashi, who separated "I did not know" from "my soul"; but again, there is just a possibility that Rashi's comment on "I did not know": "I did not know how to remain aloof from sin," was in Agnon's mind when he chose the phrase here.

"He, too, was directing" is a quotation from the prayers recited on the Day of Atonement, namely the account of the sacrificial service in the Temple: "He (the High Priest), too, directed himself so as to finish pronouncing the Name of God as they finished pronouncing their blessing."

"It was hard for them to part" reproduces the words "It is hard for me to part from you" used by Rashi in his commentary

---

[30] Possibly Agnon also recalled 2 Samuel 6:16, which has 'looked forth' and 'window' and mentions 'the Ark of the Lord' (with a different word for 'Ark'), but the context there is even less congenial.

on Leviticus 23:36 and Numbers 29:36. Both verses refer to the rites on the festival day which is added to the seven-day Festival of Tabernacles, as if God said to the celebrants: "Stay with me one day longer, it is hard for me to part from you."

The Latin phrase translates an Aramaic sentence, in which the word for 'empty' is actually Hebrew. It is taken from Kabbalah literature,[31] and frequently cited. It signifies, of course, the omnipresence of God.

"did not think of . . . and he forgot her" is a literal quotation, keeping the Biblical tenses, from Genesis 40:23 "And the chief butler did not think of (lit., did not remember) Joseph and he forgot him." These Biblical 'consecutive' tenses are rarely used by Agnon, but in our passage he uses one in the phrase "inclined her ear to listen," which is not a quotation, and introduces it (in a way found in the Bible, but not recognized by the grammars) into the quotation "she did not know her soul," where the original text has a 'simple' tense.

In view of Agnon's habit of revising his stories for each new edition, it is interesting to note that in the 1953 edition of his *Collected Stories* (cf. Hebrew text 5), only the last two items are left intact: the Aramaic phrase and the quotation from Genesis 40. The phrase "he, too, (was) directing" has the word for 'was' added, thus making it conform with modern usage. Similarly "she did not know her soul" is put into the present tense so as to agree with the historical present of 'heard.' While these usages are probably part of Agnon's desire to conform with normative grammar as presented to him by Hebrew grammarians of his acquaintance, it is significant that he did away altogether with the quotation from Judges 5, and replaced it by a new sentence: "she came and stood by the window and was peeping." Incidentally, he replaced also the phrase "and inclined her ear to listen" by the simple verb "and listened."

The phrases discussed here share with melitza the feature of being identifiable quotations. They are not ancient phrases used as modern Hebrew idioms, although they differ in the degree of source linkage, and a phrase like "she did not know her soul"

---

[31] Zohar, Section *Tikkune ha-Zohar*, paragraph 57; cf. also Y. Tishbi, *Mishnat ha-Zohar*, I (second ed., Jerusalem 1970-71), p. 511.

would qualify as idiom by its semantic structure. The others are straightforward free combinations, and could in principle have been formed without the classical source.[32] Yet these phrases are not melitza because they have in no instance any connection with the context in which the quotation appears in the original, and there is none of that interplay of original context and new context which gives melitza its flavor. Even where reference to the source would not actually spoil the effect (as it might for the quotation from Judges 5, "looked forth through the lattice"), it appears to me that it would not add anything. And yet it seems evident that the author has taken care that the phrases should be identified as quotations, by leaving Biblical tenses intact in the one from Genesis 40, and in collocating 'window' and 'lattice' in the one from Judges 5. We cannot but conclude that the source linkage must have a purpose. Since this purpose is not communicative, it must be connotative, in other words, for the purpose of creating atmosphere, or, in modern terms, a register.

The passage that appears here is a decisive one in the development of the plot. This one-time meeting, without a word being exchanged, and without face-to-face confrontation, is the turning-point in Dinah's life, the point at which she starts on the path towards becoming an ^{c}agunah, a woman whose husband has disappeared, and who by Jewish law cannot remarry. She never marries her intended bridegroom, and Ben-Uri has 'forgotten' her. The symbolism of this strange tale, like that of most other stories of Agnon's, has been hotly debated, but it appears that critics agree that this is not just a story about two people, but about matters of the spirit or the human soul. Yet, even if we take the story at its surface meaning, the archaic phrases inject into the description of the fateful meeting a dreamlike quality that belies both the simple and sparse sentences and the trite things Dinah is doing.

We may thus define the role of identifiable source-linked phrases in Agnon's usage, as distinct from linguistic material taken from the Sources in general, as that of adding another dimension to the writing. Such additional connotative dimensions are available in other languages through the use of dialect, colloquial, slang, technical jargon, religious language, archaisms, etc., all according

---

[32] As is the phrase 'inclined her ear to listen.' In the Hebrew Bible 'incline one's ear' and 'listen' frequently occur in co-ordination, but never with 'listen' subordinated.

to the special circumstances of each language community and each period. Such registers are in principle available to the modern Hebrew writer, there being social and communal differences in speech, as well as distinct registers in writing. Spoken Hebrew indeed uses transition to such registers for effect, and so do humorists and some short-story writers close to the spoken language. But literary Hebrew until recently, as we have seen, kept aloof from the spoken language, and this forced it to develop registers of its own. Attempts to create registers by varying the sources have failed, as we have seen in the case of the 'colloquial' based on Aramaic; the same is true of an earlier idea of using Mishnaic Hebrew for communicative contexts and Biblical Hebrew for the expression of sentiment. Being predominantly derived from the classical Sources, literary Hebrew can vary the degree of closeness to the Sources. Thus direct quotation becomes an equivalent of archaism. I use the term 'equivalent' in a purely structural sense; the uses of this archaizing register in Agnon's works serve quite different purposes as compared with archaism in present-day English literature, for instance.

This is clearly something quite distinct from melitza. Melitza was not a register, but a pervasive feature of style which could appear at all levels of writing. Since, as we have seen, in Agnon's quotations the original context matters little, it is also less important than in the melitza period that the exact passage in the Sources should be identified by the reader, as long as it is clear to him from what type of source the quotation comes. This applies especially to quotations from Talmud and Midrash. Scholars have been able to trace many phrases in Agnon's writings to definite Source passages by dint of intensive searching, but even a reader familiar with those Sources will identify only a minute part of them without research. Readers of this type are rare in Israel nowadays, and the vast popularity of Agnon's writings amongst educated Israelis in general proves that enjoyment of his work is not dependent on such identifications. Agnon can be read and enjoyed at different levels: anyone able to sense the register variations will get the connotations, while a person with a thorough traditional upbringing will occasionally thrill to the pleasure of recognizing a phrase.

This is not Agnon's only register. He has also the opposite of the archaic register, with strictly negative connotations. To illustrate this, we give here the translation of a passage from his posthumous novel *Shira,*[33] which describes the life of the Jerusalem university coterie (cf. Hebrew text 6):

"Once more Herbst edged his way between the closely-placed tables and the chairs that were tipped up so that their back legs stuck out, caring little that everyone was knocking against them. The very nature of a chair is that he who sits on it should sit as he wishes, without paying attention to any passers-by hurt by him. Thus Herbst once more found himself inside the coffee-house, except that on the previous occasion the latter had been sad and deserted, but now Lisbeth Neu was with him. He was, however, amazed at all those people that were sitting in the coffee-house, for they did not rise out of respect for her and did not vacate their chairs for her. Since no one offered her his chair, he began to look for a chair. He did not find a chair free. It so happened, however, that one of those who were sitting in the coffee-house arose from his chair to betake himself, be it to *a meeting or a committee-meeting, or a conference,* or maybe to his own home, and his chair became vacant."

I have tried to render by archaisms and high-register words those lexical items which are not found in normal written Hebrew. In particular I draw attention to the word translated 'coffee-house.' Agnon never used the Israeli term *bet-qaféh* for 'café' or 'coffee-shop,' but always denoted this typical Israeli institution by the form *bet-qahwah,* which he pronounced [bɛt-kávə]. Though the spelling looks like the Arabic word for 'coffee' (and is most probably derived from it) and was in use in the early stages of modern Hebrew, what Agnon no doubt meant to be read was the Polish and Hungarian pronunciation which was current in Galician Yiddish.[34] It was part of his *distancement* from Israeli Hebrew. The same novel contains another, much-discussed instance of this: Herbst's ambition to be promoted to 'full professor' is not expressed by the term current in the Hebrew University, *profesor min ha-minyan,* lit. 'professor of the statutory number,' of which Agnon was of course fully aware,[35] and which should have

---

[33] Jerusalem and Tel Aviv 1971, p. 16. The novel was published by his daughter from a manuscript on which Agnon had been working for over twenty years.

[34] Cf. Polish *kawa,* Hungarian *kávé.*

[35] It actually appears in *Shira,* p. 105, as part of a list of promotions.

appealed to him as being coined in imitation of traditional Hebrew terminology. Instead, he employs a coinage of his own, *profesor gamur,* lit. 'an absolute professor.'

In this kind of style, the three words underlined: 'meeting' 'committee-meeting' and 'conference' stand out as belonging to a different world. All three are normal literary Hebrew, and Agnon did not even include the neologism *kenes* for 'conference' (here *kinus*), which caused much controversy and thus could have attracted his attention. Of course it is entirely irrelevant to the narrative where the ex-occupant of the chair might have gone; this is just part of the negative characterization of the café crowd, as are the remarks about the tipped-up chairs of eager debaters. The irony is made complete by the final words, suggesting that such a person might possibly even spend some time in his own home. The alien terminology of meetings is heaped up in *gradatio,* and contrasts sharply with the gentle archaism and unworldliness in the description of the café. We may thus see in this a marker of a special register used by Agnon in speaking of 'alien' phenomena. This corresponds to some extent to the use of slang or argot in the work of writers identified with bourgeois society.

We have been referring to the 'Agnonic' style, Agnon's basic or neutral register, and have stated that it differs from non-literary written Hebrew and from the literary Hebrew of most of his contemporaries. The difference consists mainly in a much higher percentage of grammatical and lexical items from Mishnaic Hebrew than is found in normal written Hebrew.[36] This is not for the reasons which made J. Klausner and others prefer Mishnaic Hebrew to Biblical. Agnon did not, in fact, directly imitate Mishnaic Hebrew. His typical narrative style is derived from that of 18th-19th century East European Hassidic literature. He came from a Hassidic background, and many of his stories are set in Hassidic life of former generations. Hassidic writers used stories

[36] Some of the items in the passage discussed are: 1. *kemot* 'as' for *kemo* or *kefi*; 2. in the sentence 'it had been sad and deserted,' the word for 'had been' *hayah* comes at the end instead of the beginning; 3. *tameah hayah* (compound past) for *tamah* or, more usually, *hishtomem*; 4. *me'ahar she-* for 'since'; 5. the infinitive form *lelekh* for *lalekhet*; 5. *zaquf,* literally 'erect,' for something that protrudes horizontally; 6. *ᶜamad* 'got up,' for *qam*; 7. *iraᶜ* 'it happened,' instead of *be-miqreh,* lit. 'by accident,' in ordinary Hebrew *iraᶜ* is only used of important events; 8. the absence of a conjunction before this verb.

extensively as a means of imparting religious truths, and succeeded in creating for this purpose, out of the elements of the learned Biblical-Talmudic melitza of their period, a simple language resembling spoken Yiddish in character (and not the stilted Yiddish of 18th-century works). Agnon thus took over an idiom in which the elements from the classical Sources had already been integrated and adapted to express a modern, though not Western, pattern of thought. Of course Agnon's imitation is not a pastiche, nor based on a systematic analysis of Hassidic Hebrew, but is rather the result of familiarity with its procedures. Therefore he also can draw upon additional material from the Sources in the manner characteristic for Hassidic Hebrew.

In the past twenty years the basic pattern of Agnon's language, along with many of his mannerisms of presentation, has become popular with younger Israeli novelists and short-story writers, and seems to be establishing itself as the typical idiom of artistic prose, as opposed to non-fiction and utilitarian writing. On the other hand, the younger writers did not take over Agnon's use of direct Source quotation as register. The reason may be that they were not sufficiently aware of it; but since 'Agnonic' Hebrew itself now functions as a register, and they, in contrast to Agnon, are free to use colloquial, social dialects, and technical Hebrew for register effects, they do not need this device.

IV. *Selection As Language Development.*

The reader of the foregoing analysis may well have been asking himself by what right its author established distinctions between different assemblages of language material all taken from the same reservoir of the classical Sources. After all, the difference between them is not based on the use of Biblical Hebrew vis-à-vis Mishnaic Hebrew, or either of them vis-à-vis a mixed language, or any other feature of the Sources, such as literary genres found there. What we have here are to all appearances different random selections from one and the same mixture.

It seems that one of the reasons for the unwillingness of language planners (see note 6) to recognize registers in contemporary Hebrew is their conviction that all options are still open, so that in principle each of the present groupings might be extended to absorb the entire original Source material; hence present differences between them are irrelevant. This is also one of the more rational explanations of the designation of present-day Hebrew as a 'language in process of revival' (*lashon mithayyah*), preferred in normativist circles to calling it a living language (*lashon hayyah*).

It is true that, statistically speaking, the bulk of every type of current Hebrew is derived from the Sources. This must be understood in the sense that words do not always have the same meaning as in the Source from which they come, but they may have a meaning given to them in the Middle Ages or modern times on the basis of interpretations now recognized to be erroneous. Only in very rare cases have stubborn scholars succeeded in getting meanings in popular use changed on scientific grounds. As our understanding of Bible and Talmud improves with research, this gap between scientifically established Source meanings and modern Hebrew is likely to grow steadily. This, however, does not affect the status of such words.

Even the proportion of vocabulary taken from each Source is roughly equal in each type of Hebrew. The reason is that words found in the Bible (and which may also have formed part of Mishnaic and/or medieval Hebrew), though only ca. 10% of the total vocabulary, make up 90% of the 100 most frequent and 80% of the 1,000 most frequent words in today's language; while the proportion of Mishnaic and medieval material increases as frequency decreases, and the bulk of post-1880 neologisms is low in frequency of use. The result is that in practically any text, words found in the Bible will make up 60-70% of the vocabulary items, and 15-20% will be from Mishnaic Hebrew. Differences between registers will thus be marginal in this respect, though in effect they may be striking, such as the almost total absence of the post-1880 component in Agnon's style.

The differences are more qualitative, concerning the choice of individual items absorbed from each Source vocabulary. Though in a living language real synonyms are rare, there are many words of equal or nearly equal meaning belonging to different levels of local, social, or stylistic usage. When the language is not spoken, these differences become obliterated, and large numbers of synonyms emerge. When modern written Hebrew was established, it brought into use some of these synonyms and neglected others; when spoken Hebrew arose, it made a somewhat different choice, not as a matter of policy, but for a variety of reasons which it may be quite impossible to reconstruct. Once a selection had become established by usage, it became a linguistic system in which, in de Saussure's words, *tout se tient*. It was now subject to its own forces of preservation and of change, conditioned partly by the nature and mutual relations of the items it contained and partly by the social uses for which it was employed. This includes sources of new vocabulary formation. Spoken Hebrew absorbed foreign words, especially from English, as well as Hebrew and foreign slang; non-artistic Hebrew resisted the entry of words recognizable as coming from a living foreign language, but freely took over 'international' words and fashion words from sciences and ideologies; while literary Hebrew, besides being fertile in creating new words from Hebrew roots, also borrows from Aramaic and is much more open to new accretions from the Sources. There is also some downward seepage of vocabulary, but as yet little osmosis upwards. Even in journalese it is usual to mark colloquialisms by prefixing some excuse such as 'as they say with us.'

The different registers are clearly differentiated and easily identified by the Israeli speaker. The common Source reservoir exists as a historical fact and as a standby in normativist argumentation, but as far as I can see has no effect on the existing registers of Hebrew, which function just like the registers of any other language. The reservoir comes into play once more in the creation of technical registers and also when a new literary register is introduced into the language, as was the case with the language Agnon used. Then, so to say, there is a new shake out of the bag. Something approaching this idea was stated by Bialik in 1932:[37] "the writer . . . has to descend into the ancient mines of the language in order to mine there for himself the linguistic material which he requires. The raw material of all layers and periods down to the deepest strata will once more be thrown into the melting-pot, to cast from it a new-old language, tied by a thousand fine invisible threads to its former life strands." The new selection, however, is not random, for it has to be carried out with a tendency towards maximum differentiation vis-à-vis existing reservoirs. This need to differentiate is indeed proof for the existence of registers in the minds of Hebrew speakers in Palestine as early as 1908, when *^cAgunot* first appeared. This is a span of less

---

[37]*Leshonenu* 4 (1931-2) 324-5.

than one full generation after the beginning of the revival of Hebrew.

This selection by differentiation is a feature of the development of all modern languages with a classical basis, such as Arabic, Persian, Tamil, etc. Although none of these was revived in the sense of having a spoken dimension *added* to it, they have had registers added in the course of modernization and westernization. They share with Hebrew the characteristic that they possess a large traditional literature still widely read and taught, and therefore available as a reservoir for developing the language. Daily papers, modern novel-writing, and above all technical subjects, have acquired their effective and distinctive styles by such shakes out of the bag. The creation of a technical vocabulary in Arabic, for example, has reactivated many hundreds of ancient words.

It would be wrong, however, to treat this process as a special feature of revived classical languages. What gives that impression is the visible existence of the reservoir in the form of books, coupled with the consciousness of that ancient literature as something separate from the language as actually in use. In languages such as English, where most of the older literature is read in its original form only by specialists, it appears to us that for any development the language is thrown upon its resources as existing here and now, or upon borrowing. But the facts of language development show that in these cases, too, there is a reservoir formed of the colloquial, local varieties, technical sub-languages, and to some extent also obsolete words from earlier literature, as made available through dictionaries and specialist research. The successful revival of words such as English 'sibling' shows that long-obsolete words still lead something like a semi-existence. Here is the sociolinguistic base for the purist word-revivals in so many languages. Literature also revives linguistic material. Sir Walter Scott may have intended his medieval words to serve as milieu markers only, but at least some of them were reactivated as a result of the popularity of his works. German writers of the 18th and early 19th centuries revived many words which were by then obsolete.[38] What makes such revivals possible is not merely the positive attitude of the educated reader to words he knows to have come from his own

---

[38]Cf. W. Kuhberg, *Verschollenes Sprachgut und seine Wiederbelebung in neuhochdeutscher Zeit* (Frankfurt am Main 1933).

language, but also the fact that after phonetic modernization their structure resembles that of words still alive. In the case of revived classical languages, where the spelling is historical, the structural similarity is even more obvious.

Nor must we attach too much weight to the idea that in societies using a classical revived language the educated reader has direct access to the ancient sources, and is thus likely to have met the reactivated words before. In this matter the differences between classical and non-classical languages are not so clear-cut. Educated English speakers will generally be familiar with Shakespeare, while educated Italians still read Dante. On the other hand, the new technical intelligentsia of the societies with classical languages are often unable to understand the old literary texts.

We might say that all natural languages possess, besides their active stock of forms and words, a reservoir on which they can draw for special purposes. The nature of this reservoir in each particular case is determined by sociolinguistic factors.

Hebrew text 1.

Yehuda ha-Levi

צֹפַּי לָךְ בִּיְשֵׁר וְנֶאֱמָנוּ   יוֹם קוֹל יַתְּבּוּ

פְּעָמֵי מַרְכְּבוֹתַי וְנֶעְצָרוּ   הֵן אִם אֲחָרִי

נְחוּמַי עֲלֵיכֶם וְנִגְבְּרוּ   יַחַד נִכְמָרוּ

Hebrew text 2.

Bialik, Ha-Matmid.

הַדְּרוֹר תָּעִיר קִנָּהּ — בַּגְּיָהּ הָרַפִּים,

לְתַגּוֹת תְּהִלַת הַשֶּׁמֶשׁ הַפְּדִיבָה,

אֶת־צִדְקַת פִּזְרוֹנָהּ בְּיוֹשְׁבֵי מַחֲשַׁפִּים:

Hebrew text 3.

S. Y. Agnon, <u>Agunot</u> 1921.

שמעה דינה בת ר' אחיעזר, אל החלון נצבה דינה
היפהפיה. בעד האשנב השקיפה ותט אזן לשמוע ולבה נמשך
אל בית המלאכה כמו על ידי כשפים רחמנא ליצלן.
ירדה דינה לראות את מעשי האומן, היא ונערותיה
עמה. נתנה עיניה בארון, בחשה את הסממנים, בדקה את
הקישוטין ונמלה את הכלים ובן־אורי עושה את מעשהו,
מקציע חוליה מן התיבה ושר, מקציע ושר. שומעת דינה
קולו ולא תדע נפשה. ואף הוא מכֵּוֵן קולו להמשיך לבה
בנגינתו, שתהא עומדת כאן ולא תזוז לעולם. לבם נהנה
וחרד. קשה עליהם הפרידה.
אבל משנתעסק בן־אורי במלאכתו יותר, דבק דבק
במלאכתו. עיניו ולבו נתובים לארון הקודש, לית אתר
פנוי מיניה. ולא זכר בן־אורי את דינה וישכחה.

Hebrew text 4.

S. Y. Agnon, <u>Agunot</u> 1908.

שמעה אותה דינה, בתו יחידתו של הקצין — ונתדבקה
בשמתה בנגינה זו. אל החלון נצבה דינה היפהפיה מרכינה
ראש ומטה אזן שתהא סופגת כל קול והברה העולה מלמטה.
ולבה נמשך ונמשך כמו ע"י כשפים, ר"ל ...
התחילה דינה יורדת אליו לראות גם במעשיו של האומן
ולהסתכל בהם, ונערותיה מלוות אותה לשם. שומעת היא בזמירתו
ונפשה אליו תכלה ... ואף הוא כאלו הוא מתכון להמשיך אותה
בנגינתו יותר ויותר, שתהא עומדת כאן עוד ועוד ולא תפרד
מעליו לעולם ... ושניהם לבם ירא וחרד ונבהה כאחד, כמו
שעומד כנגד אורה של הדליקה — וקשה עליהם הפרידה.
אבל לסוף התפרד הרא ממנה.
לא שהרהר זה זה בתשובה וראה שבתולה זו אינה מזומנת
בשבילו ואינה עומדת להכבס עמו לחופה. אלא עבודה זו, עבודת
הקדש, זוהי שהצילה אותו מהרהורי עבירה ומלהַתֵּר אחרי לבבו;
כי מכירון שהתחיל מתעסק במלאכתו בעשתה המלאכה עצמה יקרה לו
מכל, והשקיע בה כל נשמתו ונעשו לבו ומחשבתו ונגיבתו נתובים
בתורבים כלם כאחד רק לארון הקדש, ביום ובלילה.
כל חיי רוחו נצטמצמו ונכבסו בארון זה, שהיה נראה לו
בשמים ממעל ובארץ מתחת ואין לו עוד סלבדו בעולם כלל ...

178

Hebrew text 5.

S. Y. Agnon, <u>Agunot</u> 1953.

שמעה דינה בתו של ר' אחיעזר, באה ועמדה בחלון והיתה
מציצה ושומעת ולבה התחיל נמשך אל בית המלאכה כמו על
ידי כשפים רחמנא ליצלן . אף היא ירדה לראות את מעשי
האומן, היא ונערותיה עמה, ונסתכלה בארון ובחשה את
הסמטנים ובדקה את הקישוטין ונטלה את הכלים ובן אורי
היה עושה את מעשהו, מקציע חוליא מן התיבה ושר, מקציע
ושר. שומעת דינה קולו ואיבה יודעת בפשה . ואף הוא
היה מכוין קולו להמשיך לבה בנגינתו שתהא עומדת כאן
ולא תזוז לעולם . אבל משנתעסק בן אורי במלאכתו ירתר
נתדבק במלאכתו, עד שהיו עיניו ולבו נתונים לארון
הקודש, לית אתר פנוי מיניה . ולא זכר בן אורי את
דינה וישכחה.

Hebrew text 6.

S. Y. Agnon, <u>Shira</u>.

ושוב נדחק הרבסם בין השולחנות הצפופים והכסאות שרגליהם
האחוריות זקופות ולא איכפת להן שהכל נתקלים בהן. כל
עיקרו של כסא שהיושב עליו ישב לו כמות שהוא רוצה ואינו
נותן דעתו בעוברים ושבים שנפגעים על ידו. בכן שוב
נמצא הרבסם בתוך בית הקהוה, אלא שבראשונה עצוב ונעזב
היה ועכשיו היתה ליסבט ביי עמו. אבל תמיה היה על כל
יושבי בית הקהוה שאינם עומדים לכבודה ואינם מפנים לה
את כסאותיהם. מאחר שלא הציע לה אדם את כסאו התחיל
מבקש לה כסא. לא מצא כסא פנוי. אירע שאחד מיושבי
בית הקהוה עמד מכסאו כדי לילך לו, אם לאספה או לישיבה
או לכינוס או אולי לביתו ונתפנה כסאו.

179

SUMMARY COMMENTARY

Judah Goldin

Such a session as this may or may not provide an adequate summary, for we have had a number of papers, interrelated but not necessarily interconnected. But one thing it can do, and that is, serve as illustration of what happens with the handing down of texts and the rise of versions. We were all sent copies of the papers: these would have been text, at least tentative text. The authors of these papers then presented oral summaries of what they had written. Then came commentaries followed by discussions of the summaries and the papers; and now we are having two additional summaries this morning. How close is all this to the original papers?

Last night when we were at the Papers' house, Mr. Marckwardt and I wondered whether we should divide the subject matter, one of us covering one group of essays and the other another group. We decided against this plan; instead we would come freewheeling, responding to what was most congenial to each of us. It might be interesting, then, not only to compare the summaries with the originals, but summary with summary. In the meantime the authors and commentators themselves may very likely want to revise their original drafts. Although what was said is not completely beyond recovery, recovery will inevitably involve problems of transmission, collation, revision, and, with living authors, consulting. We are already deep in the business of editing.

Something occurred after the last paper yesterday afternoon which must have been noted by everyone present. We had been going along for two days, following the program faithfully: there was discussion of the problem of deciphering an ancient text, of the nature of linguistic evidence, and of various problems connected with ancient literature. We then moved on to modern texts, modern literature, and even to the literature of non-texts, of societies with scripts and without scripts (as Mr. Austerlitz put it). I think there was a quiet realization that the linguists were going their way and the text men theirs. And after the last paper, suddenly, possibly unexpectedly, reactions like these followed: "But aren't we really one?" "Isn't it a fact that the philologists and the linguists are two sides of the same coin?"

I think we may be, but I think that the reconciliation came too quickly. For what is the situation at present? Unfortunately our specializations keep compelling us—even when we wish to be more receptive—to focus for the most part on the materials and methods to which we have devoted ourselves for many years. It is not just a question of time, it is a question of habit. And this is an aspect of professionalization, true very likely even before the development of Alexandrian scholarship. Exchanges, to be effective, must be more rather than less sustained. I doubt if they are except in very rare instances.

It may indeed be—it very likely will be before long—that reconciliation between linguistics experts and textual scholars will take place, but it won't occur as trigger-reconciliation. What happened yesterday, I suspect, happened because of a sudden fear that if we drift much further apart, what we do may cease to have meaning, that is, cease to be comprehensible by any but the practitioners themselves. The word 'meaning' is a dangerous one, and in some quarters is almost a dirty word, because it is often used fuzzily. Very well. But the discovery of formal units and patterns in linguistic behavior, and the study of what men have said and say as they try to express themselves in a historical context, cannot be unrelated to each other. If so, expectations are not unrealistic. To be sure, there are risks (especially of the tyranny of preconceptions); but there are always risks. There is no choice, really. We cannot come empty-handed and empty-headed toward the investigations we want to make, whether we are dealing with the nature of language as such or the contents of documents.

This was felt, and said, and that's to the good. It was good to be reminded by Mr. Gelb that before Champollion began his deciphering he had already immersed himself thoroughly in such things as Egyptian history and Egyptian religion in order to come to the conclusion that he was dealing with a language, signs of a language, rather than just magical signs. Preparation (= learning and trained intelligence) is called for in recovering not only a language, or the significance of an ancient text, but also a modern one. Agnon demands an education, as Mr. Rabin observed.

Mr. Bailey said something at the end of his paper—it was said so quietly, I hope we don't disregard it—after his illustration of the difficulty of recovering a text. Beware of trying to edit a text, he said, unless you know your Greek and Latin well. What can be more self-evident, someone who has not read his paper might say. Yet, how important that is, I think everyone of us has discovered in seminars when he has dealt, for example, with first and second year graduate students to whom some text has been given to re-construct. Occasionally one is tempted to admit that the suggested reconstruction is even an improvement of the original. But our group here hardly needs to be reminded of the history of textual emendations in several literatures. The task of editing a text, as of recovering a language about to disappear (as Ms. Haas made clear), means that you cannot come with a simple hearing-aid.

As for the changing meaning and complexion of terms in the language itself: we need the lexicons, we need the concordances, but in the end they are not substitutes for reading, reading, and rereading. Mr. Merkelbach asks, "Have you noticed the number of terms the Christians appropriated from the world of sports?" Not only a lingo but a popular social pastime and enthusiasm have here been recovered. A question might still remain: to what extent is the user of such vocabulary conscious of the specific origin of his terms, and to what extent have the terms been completely neutralized by his time, so that no vivid imagery survives in his mind? When I speak of a goal, do I have a chariot-race in mind or a football game? But the point is that we are not speaking of a word or two, but rather of whole clusters of expression. And this awareness comes only from close and continuous reading. It might come from a computer; but without an anticipatory suspicion, what shall we feed the computer?

I would like to return to several other observations on words shortly.

Since we talked a good deal about editing, perhaps the follow-ing trivial incident has some interest. The other night one of our lecturers and I had dinner in the restaurant here, and a young girl, a student at the university, was our waitress. We were also joined by two colleagues. When I got my bill from the young lady, I noticed that for 'dessert' she wrote d-e-s-e-r-t. I asked my com-panion to show me his bill, because I wanted to see whether what was written on mine was just a slip. But his bill also read d-e-s-e-r-t.

Will a papyrologist someday correct the spelling, or will he know that the word is misspelled not only at the University of Michigan but on every campus, in other words, not just at hamburger stands on highways? When is something like this a misspelling and when does it become an acceptable variant? The question, of course, goes beyond spelling, nor is it a new one. Since in the 17th century one did write d-e-s-e-r-t, is this a sign that all norms are not only relative but futile? Despite the contemporary assault on 'as' by 'like,' are we to assume that if we find such an example in an author of an earlier century, it must be a mistake— or is it a prophecy?

One feature of words which might be touched on is that of 'loanwords.' Sometimes it is invoked as an indication of the failure of a language to provide for itself, so to speak. In my opinion it is rather a sign of the self-confidence and vitality of a language, of the language-users. Experience suddenly outruns available vocabulary; people using that language begin to appropriate and naturalize for their own needs. You get loanwords when two cultures are neighbors, friendly or otherwise, as everyone knows. The word 'Sanhedrin' is even the title of a treatise of the Talmud, though Hebrew has no difficulty saying 'high court' *bet din ha-gadol.* But there is a more striking illustration. There's no lack of terms in Hebrew for 'to praise.' Yet in post-biblical Hebrew the root *qls* appears with that meaning. Who would expect it, knowing that that root in Ezekiel means 'to scoff, to deride'? Yet S. Lieberman demonstrated that the post-biblical term was to be related to the Greek *kalôs, kalôs,* a term used in hailing the Emperor. For the Jews this was attractive—to express one's awe and loyalty to God. The term said precisely for them what they felt the familiar Hebrew had not quite expressed. Such borrowings are a form of inventiveness.

There is of course a counterpart to loanwords, and that is the death of words. I owe this observation to W. H. Auden, who said in one of his essays that his was probably the last generation in which you could use the word 'fairy' and mean fairy. One cannot write to a dear friend any longer and say, "I hope you're having a gay time," without embarrassment. *Hitmasser* is fine modern and even medieval Hebrew for 'devote oneself to.' In contemporary slang (in the feminine), it's another story. This goes on in every living language.

Shifts need not be from life to death, or from borrowing to adopting, as though they were the whole story. Within a language, different meanings develop for the same word, and *inside the texts* the more-than-one meaning persists. When the lexicons have not yet caught up with the phenomenon, one is left on his own. This, I submit, is one of the most serious difficulties with understanding the Hebrew Bible. For the Old Testament is a collection of writings of over a millennium. Is the meaning of words in the age of Deborah, for example, that of the author (or translator) of Ecclesiastes? H. L. Ginsberg, who (along with F. Zimmerman) argued for the present Hebrew text of Ecclesiastes being a translation from Aramaic, has pointed out that $^c amal$ in this book is not 'toil' but 'gain.' That is certainly not its meaning in (let us say) Jeremiah 20:18.

Knowledge of Semitic languages—as the medieval Jewish commentators also were aware, but they did not pursue this course consistently or systematically, and could not have a knowledge of cuneiform languages—such knowledge has enriched our understanding of the vocabulary of biblical Hebrew. Hence the study of these in Old Testament studies has been popular in modern times. But Mr. Barr raises and emphasizes still another very important question: "How far does the text (we have) give accurate evidence of the language in which it was written?"

Shifts in meaning go on everywhere. Let me give one example from post-biblical Hebrew, to illustrate that while meanings are fluid, words tend to be conservative. *Gemillut* (or possibly *gemillot*) *ḥasadim* in the sources stands so firmly for 'acts of lovingkindness,' in other words, acts of one man's generosity to another, it is surprising to discern that at first it expressed piety towards God. The 'humanistic' value does not replace the old expression; it retains it.

In this connection I would like to say a word about ancient commentaries. I admit I'm thinking principally of Midrash, but this can apply to Church Fathers and medieval exegesis no less. Everyone has observed again and again that these works offer interpretations that are anachronistic. Hence the attitude that they cannot be taken seriously for purposes of literal interpretation. No one denies that they are valuable reflections of their own time; it is the value for explaining the original that is rejected. If it were simply individual words or clauses, perhaps there would be little disagreement about the matter. But speaking specifically of Midrash, I would like to suggest that this is an oversimplification. Not only do some *midrashim* preserve accurate renditions (see in this connection S. Lieberman's *Hellenism in Jewish Palestine*), but the very homiletical explanations of a single verse reveal, quite frequently, what is actually reflected by the biblical section or pericope as a whole, which without that homiletical observation might have been missed. I could offer many examples, but one will do: I deliberately choose an extreme one. A third century (A.D.) teacher, R. Levi, says boldly that the interrogative statement of Genesis 18:25, "Shall not the judge of the whole earth practise justice," is to be understood as a declarative, "The judge of the whole earth is *not* to practise justice," that is, he is to practise mercy.

Clearly the exegesis reveals that R. Levi is more concerned with a moral than with syntax. Strange to say, however, that very view reflects not only R. Levi's personal message (obviously), but something of the character of that Genesis section—and that is the point. For a re-examination of the whole Genesis passage does demonstrate that nothing like the concept of strict justice, as the ancients would have argued arithmetically, is resorted to there. In other words, although R. Levi's interpretation is certainly not literal, nevertheless it is not as alien to the biblical *theme* as one might have expected at first. (Naturally I don't deny that, like rhetors, the ancient Midrashic savants can make a text stand on its head.)

Perhaps it is not superfluous to add that in the history of culture it is anachronism that often made it possible for ancient texts to survive, because by reinterpretation people made those texts relevant to their needs and thoughts. So they read and preserved. For folklorists especially this could prove a fruitful field of investitation. When the ancient is saved, how far is it transformed by a later generation and how far does it influence that generation? Or, what is the dialectical relation between the two?

Ambiguity of evidence is constant. Again something everyone of us encounters; nevertheless one example may be in order. The series of paintings—panels and registers—in the Dura Europos synagogue of the third century A.D. include one scene of the Pharaoh's daughter and her maidservants discovering the baby Moses in the Nile. The princess (or possibly one of her maidservants) is presented frontally naked in the water. A late friend of mine and scholar was studying those pictures closely because he felt that they validated an important theory of his. In order to study the pictures thoroughly, he had them enlarged, and as a result many details that would have escaped the eye now stood out boldly. They established his case, he felt. It turned out, however, that *in situ* the scene of the Pharaoh's daughter with Moses could not have been seen clearly, if at all, by the worshippers in the synagogue. Even more to the point, bathing naked in the water means no more than just that, bathing—for how else did the ancients bathe: surely without bathing suits, as E. J. Bickerman has already observed. The case therefore was anything but established. The specificity of detail in that representation is not to be gainsaid; the photo is unmistakable; but the evidence has been disproportionately magnified. Would this have happened if the scholar had not started with a theory to vindicate? Possibly no, but then again possibly yes. Come to data with nothing and you are likely to get nothing.

All such problems, we have learned again in these meetings, are not confined to ancient materials. It is not only difficult but futile to expect a perfect text (edition), even 19th century ones, as Mr. Peckham illustrated. We have heard what it is like trying to put Mark Twain in shape, and not only Mark Twain. But though a perfect edition is impossible, a bad one is very possible. Due to carelessness, needless to say. But it may well be the result of starting too soon, before sufficient data are available, and deciding on the basis of what is simply available at the moment. (Yet, what other moments have we?) For years people were making corrections in Palestinian Hebrew texts on the basis of the orthography familiar to them from the Babylonian Talmud. And orthography affected understanding. It was L. Ginzberg who (first?) called attention early in this century to the evidence that in manuscripts of Palestinian sources, a number of spellings varied "consistently" and were not to be corrected (for example, the word for 'man' appears as *'adn,* not *'adm*). In texts he has edited, L. Finkelstein has shown when a variant is an independent variant and when only a feature of a family of manuscripts. P. Maas has been the guide to a host of scholars. A manuscript variant may well be a windfall (and also not!), but the same may be said of a reading which a careful medieval authority quotes from an ancient source. Further, if a classical interpretation is ignored by a medieval commentator, that may well be a signal of the dismissal of an accepted interpretation. Such testimony is not to be underestimated.

Approaches to problems also became things of fashion. In our time in biblical studies, Gunkel's *Sitz im Leben* is invoked repeatedly. In his own day it took a long time for him to get a sympathetic hearing. Nowadays Ugaritic traces are sometimes discovered with a frequency that is nothing less than astonishing. And this is not altogether the result of accession of new knowledge. Such things have happened before (and will happen again), as the epigrammatic *Bibel und Babel* can remind us.

A tension between linguists and philologians exists, and I'm not sure that that's necessarily bad. Perhaps it serves to put both groups on their guard, to recognize that human expression—that is, the way language develops or behaves, and the uses to which it is put in literature (what people take the trouble to write down with the hope that it will be saved for a long or short time)—demands more than one discipline. The tension persists, for in the meantime we are involved in mastering the multiplicity of details in respective fields if generalizations are not to be idle, and because mastery of new methods is also a slow process.

A brief summary of what a number of people have said unavoidably omits. And the summarizer may put a stress where the speakers would have preferred an unstressed sentence. So too in reverse, inadequate emphasis of what deserves more emphasis. Above all, by selecting illustrations from his own materials, the summarizer may unwittingly convert one set of concerns into another set. Summary itself may, therefore, become response or commentary or even misreading. Mr. Marckwardt will doubtless put things differently and restore balance. Since I've drawn on Midrash, permit me to close with it as a figure of speech. The Midrash says that a biblical verse may have 49 faces, that is, 7 times 7 possibilities. Of course that's supposed to apply to divinely revealed words. But the human word too has its faces of interpretation. Whether the materials in texts and languages have 7 times 7 aspects, I don't know; maybe they have more, maybe fewer. But they certainly have more than one.

SUMMARY COMMENTARY

Albert H. Marckwardt †

Since Mr. Goldin and I are sharing the task of summarizing the preceding four sessions, I should like to begin my remarks with a reference to the commentary he has just concluded. It is significant, I believe, that he began it by referring to the topic which occupied much of our attention late yesterday afternoon, which in turn reflects the question or issue which gave rise to this entire conference, namely the respective roles, the domains of the philologist and the linguist. In short, the wheel has come full circle.

Throughout the conference as a whole as well as in connection with the summary just concluded, it has been easy for me to think of instances drawn from English philology and linguistics which would serve as apt illustrations of points which were being made in connection with matters far afield. For example, yesterday afternoon Mr. Austerlitz spoke of the time when the competent philologist-comparativist and the general linguist-theoretician could co-exist in the same person, mentioning as examples Whitney, Boas, Sapir, and Leonard Bloomfield. To this distinguished list I would add Thomas Lounsbury of Yale, George Philip Krapp of Columbia, George McKnight of Ohio State, and George Hempl and Samuel Moore of Michigan.

Recently I have been working on a history of the development of linguistic studies at the University of Michigan, which has given me an opportunity to look into the relationship between philology and linguistics in some detail. Whereas in some institutions what is now recognized as linguistics developed as an extension of research in anthropology, at Michigan it grew primarily out of activity in the field of comparative philology. As early as 1862, Professor Edward Payne Evans was listed in the university catalogue as giving a course in the General Principles of Germanic Philology. This was two years before William Dwight Whitney delivered his six Smithsonian lectures "On the Principles of

189

Linguistic Science," and five years before they appeared in published form. In this same connection it is interesting to note that Professor George Hempl's academic title during the last nine years of his seventeen-year career at Michigan was 'Professor of English Philology and General Linguistics.' What better evidence of co-existence could one adduce? If I had to select one person of my own academic generation who combined the two functions with distinction, it would be Professor W. Freeman Twaddell of Brown University—a competent Goethe scholar on the one hand, but also concerned not only with theoretical principles of language structure, but with the application of these to the history of the Germanic languages.

At the same time it must be conceded that our discussions here of the present function and role of the linguist and the philologist fell somewhat short of reaching a general consensus; partly, I believe, because some of the time we were talking about purpose and interest, part of the time about the nature of the material that is being dealt with, and part of the time about the methods to be pursued in handling that material. The focus shifted rather frequently from one to another of these.

There are, in addition, two or three other relevant factors which, in the course of our discussions, were barely suggested but not developed. One of these was what Ms. Haas called a time-lag in the general acceptance of the term 'linguistics.' Mr. Pulgram seemed to offer support for this by his comment that he began his career at Michigan in a Department of Romance Philology and is still in the same department but with the title Professor of Romance Linguistics. Mr. Gerber reported that at the University of Iowa 'linguistics' is the current term and that 'philology' is rarely used. He wondered whether the reverse was true anywhere. I can report from personal experience that it is. Up to the time of my retirement from Princeton two years ago, very few of my colleagues in the English Department ever used the term 'linguistics.' They always talked about 'philology,' no matter what aspect or approach to the study of language was under discussion—and this despite the existence of an interdepartmental program in linguistics, to which the Department of English was a contributing member.

Another reason for the separation of linguistics and philology and the consequent rarity of the two functions existing in the same person is simply the proliferation of knowledge and scholarship in each field. At one point in the conference there was a brief comment to the effect that at meetings of learned organizations we no longer listen to papers in subdivisions of our general field other than our own; we confine ourselves to our individual areas of specialization. For four of the five decades of its existence, the Linguistic Society of America met only in general sessions. In 1962, when I gave my presidential address and was trying to look into the future, I prophesied that within a few years specialized sections would be meeting concurrently, that there would be resistance to the idea but that it would happen anyway—and of course it has.

Nor have the scholars in linguistics and philology always written with grace and clarity. Linguistics has developed not one but several terminologies of its own, and often employs a kind of algebra to accompany them. This can be forbidding to the nonspecialist.

Not mentioned in the discussion yesterday afternoon but nevertheless important is the different meaning given to the two terms in Britain and America. Let me invite a comparison here between two dictionary definitions, one from each country. First I cite the definition of 'linguistics' in the 1934 edition of Webster's *New International Dictionary:* "The study of human speech in all its aspects, including the origin, nature, structure, and modification of language or languages, including especially phonetics, phonology, morphology, accent, syntax, semantics, general or philosophical grammar, the relation between writing and speech. Called also linguistic science, science of language." It should be noted that the general editor, who ultimately reviewed all of the definitions, was Thomas A. Knott, who had been a Professor of English at the University of Iowa with specialization in the field of language and who, later in his career, came to the University of Michigan as editor of the *Middle English Dictionary.*

It is instructive to compare the definition of 'linguistics' in Webster with that of 'philology' in the 1938 edition of the *Universal Dictionary of the English Language,* edited by Henry Cecil Wyld, Merton Professor of English Language and Literature at Oxford. It begins with an archaic meaning: "The lore and pursuit of learning and literature." The principal definition follows: "Linguistic science; study of the nature and development of language, or of a given language, and of the principles which determine them." In effect, this definition of 'philology' covers precisely the same territory as the Webster definition of 'linguistics,' though in a more condensed fashion.

This raises the question as to what each of the two dictionaries does with the other term. The Webster dictionaries, both 1934 and 1961, define 'philology' much as Mr. Austerlitz dealt with it in his paper, with a knowledge of the culture as the primary goal. But, to the *Universal Dictionary*, 'linguistics' is "philology, especially that side which has to do with phonetics and changes of sound." In this general connection it should be observed that the Philological Society in England is in a very real sense the counterpart of the Linguistic Society of America, much closer to it in field and interest than it is to the American Philological Association. In short, we are in danger of being confused by labels, and we must be careful to look at the reality beneath.

As I have remarked, the broad impetus of this conference grew out of our concern for the respective roles of linguist and philologist. Naturally the specific topic, *Language and Texts: the Nature of Linguistic Evidence,* grew out of this concern; but when we framed the topic, we were not at all by implication confining the role or area of interest of either the philologist or the linguist. It was not our feeling that the principal task of the philologist was that of editor, nor did we believe that linguistic concepts had little or no relevance for editorial techniques. In fact, we believed that they did.

As a case in point, Mr. Gerber spoke yesterday of the chaotic punctuation in much of the work of Mark Twain, making it very difficult for an editor to determine principles to which he might consistently adhere. Yet the penultimate doctoral dissertation I directed at Princeton was one which had to do with the development of Mark Twain's voice or styles. The investigator chose *Innocents Abroad* as the first work to be analyzed. In it Twain in essence assumed two roles, that of a traveloguer on the one hand, and on the other that of a satirical commentator on promotional travel literature and travel narrative. A comparison of the punctuation in passages representing each of the two roles or *personae* suggests that in many instances the punctuation has been consciously manipulated to fit the role. I offer this as one instance of an area where analysis on a rigorous linguistic basis appears to have a definite bearing on the work of an editor seeking to improve this text.

In our discussions, during the past few days, of the task of the editor, we did not resolve, nor could we have been expected to, the question of the aims or purposes of an edition. My notes on this particular topic are replete with adjectives suggesting the kind of text that the editor is trying to reproduce: 'eclectic,' 'authentic,' 'definitive' among others, and just a few moments ago someone spoke of a 'perfect' text. At the same time we heard Mr. Peckham argue that in view of the masses of exemplars of any one work in this age of the printed book and photographic reprints, editing in the time-honored and conventional manner has become something of a futile exercise.

Yet the problem besetting an editor faced with thousands of copies in numerous printings and editions is not necessarily different from that confronting the linguist when he sets out to make a survey of a widely-spoken language. He, too, has before him a body of data which literally overwhelms the imagination. Let us take the English language as a case in point. At the present time there are approximately 275,000,000 native speakers. It has been estimated that on the average each one of us speaks approximately 50,000 words every week. Multiplying the two numbers gives us the total number of English words spoken in just a single week. (This still excludes everything that is written, as well as the total usage of non-native speakers.) I shall not trouble you with the array of zeros resulting from this multiplication, but suffice it to say the figure is in the trillions, and when broken down it amounts to approximately a billion words per minute. In the light of this, one of the largest and most carefully selected samplings of English that we have, the Brown University Corpus, consisting of 1,000,000 words appearing in print in 1961, seems infinitesimal by comparison—only a fraction of what is being uttered in the English language every minute we are talking.

Let us look now at the other side of the coin. The problems that confront the editor of a selection which exists in but a single manuscript, such as the Old English poem *Beowulf,* do not differ materially from those which face the scholar who is trying to describe a language or decipher a script which has been preserved only in fragments, as for example Tocharian or Minoan Linear B. With languages which are still extant, but only barely so, there is the celebrated case of Morris Swadesh, whose doctoral dissertation dealt with Chitimacha, an American Indian language only two speakers of which were to be found. They did not use it, however, in identical fashion; so Swadesh had to consider one of them the speaker of the standard language and the other as representative of a dialect variant. Essentially there is little or no difference between these situations and the single-manuscript text; both require reconstruction according to something of a paleontological model.

With respect to the organization of this conference, it is notable that we vaulted from the ancient to the modern world in what seemed to be a single leap, with little consideration of what lies between the two, namely the Middle Ages and the Renaissance. It is possible that the sponsoring organization, the *Center for Coördination of Ancient and Modern Studies,* conditioned both our thinking and the emphasis of the program. There is also here at the University of Michigan a *Medieval-Renaissance Collegium.* Had it undertaken the symposium, things might have been different.

At any rate, time after time during the course of these past two days I have been reminded of striking parallels in the development of English, especially in the Middle Ages and the Renaissance, to points which a number of speakers made in their papers. For example, Mr. Merkelbach spoke of the adaptation and changes in meaning of Greek words at the time of the introduction of Christianity. Certainly the adjustment of the English lexicon to the equally strong challenge posed by the conversion of Angles and Saxons bears a strong resemblance to what happened in Greece. Words like *halga* 'saint,' *Ēaster,* and even *God* changed in meaning, conforming to the necessities imposed by the new religion. Just this morning the adoption of loanwords was mentioned, again in connection with the introduction of Christianity. This, too, was an important element in the development of the English lexicon, fulfilling precisely the same need. Not only was there direct borrowing on a significant scale, but also loan-translation, as in the case of *Gōdspel* 'gospel,' and suffixal derivation, as in ∂ryness 'three-ness,' the Old English word for *Trinity.*

We also dealt this morning with the other side of the lexical picture; Mr. Goldin remarked about the fascination of the dying out or disappearance of words from the language. It is an intriguing process, of course, and one that is much harder to recapture from the sources of information at our disposal, at least as far as English is concerned. Two types of lexical obsolescence or disappearance have come to my attention. In the one instance, we tend to use certain words in ever more and more restricted contexts. I doubt that anyone here has ever heard or read the word 'fettle' when it was not preceded by the adjective 'fine.' Current use of the word is limited to this one set phrase. Yet the *Oxford English Dictionary* records it used with the modifier 'good' as late as 1857, 'poor' as recently as 1850, and without a modifier in 1829.

Another phenomenon which occurs in English, as well as in many of the other languages under discussion here, is that of the preservation of certain words only as elements in compound formations. *Nēat,* the Old English word for cattle, occurs today chiefly in the combination 'neatsfoot oil.' The only two preservations of Old English *wer* 'man,' cognate with Latin *vir,* are in *werewolf* and the archaism *wergild.* The remaining remnants of Old English *gār* 'spear' are to be found in 'garlic, garfish, garpike.'

The proliferation of editorial apparatus as the editing of texts goes on, mentioned by Mr. Gragg, has its English counterpart in Kemp Malone's edition of *Deor's Lament,* an Old English poem of 42 lines; the edition runs to 42 pages. A recent edition of the *Battle of Brunanburh* would average out at even more than one page of apparatus per line of text.

The language of the Authorized Version of the Bible presents a parallel, in a minor way true enough, to Mr. Barr's observation about the Hebrew text. First of all, although the date (1611-1613) is contemporary with the end of Shakespeare's play-writing career, it reflects a stage of the language much earlier than that which is to be found in most of the literature of the time. There are at least two reasons for this. First of all, the translators were instructed to follow the Bishops' Bible (1568) and to alter it as little as the truth to the original would permit; and in their turn, the bishops had been enjoined to model their work on the Great Bible (1539), "and not to recede from it, but where it varyeth manifestly from the Hebrew or Greek original." This, in itself, established a time-lag of some seventy years.

Another factor with some bearing on the matter was, as H. L. Mencken pointed out some years ago, the age of the translators, which averaged over sixty. He then went on to comment that had they been forty, they would have made it lyric; as it was, they made it epic. Moreover, the relationship of the Authorized Version to the reading tradition is clear. The very title page bears the legend, "Appointed to be read in churches," and the language was unquestionably manipulated with that end in mind.

Yesterday afternoon Ms. Haas spoke of the difficulties of recapturing from field notes the pronunciation of various American Indian languages. This, too, has a parallel in the effort to determine the pronunciation of English, especially during the period from 1450 to 1750. Today we lean heavily upon the interpretation of spellings which are a departure from the rather loosely adhered-to orthographic conventions of the time. Professor Henry Cecil Wyld, whom I mentioned earlier as the editor of the *Universal Dictionary of the English Language,* deserves much of the credit for exploiting evidence of this nature. His *History of Modern Colloquial English* is an important milestone in the attempt to recapture the details of the Early Modern English sound system.

This was also a time of spelling reform; there were numerous efforts in this direction. These generally took one of two possible guises. The first was an effort to make the spelling conventions somewhat more consistent, but to disturb the existing patterns as little as possible—something like the Simplified Spelling Board of the early years of this century. The other tendency was to develop an alphabet that was essentially phonetic in nature, creating new characters when necessary, abandoning old ones when they seemed superfluous. In essence this looked forward to the development of something like the International Phonetic Alphabet. Unfortunately, any interpretation of the phonetic orthographies developed at the time is necessarily somewhat circular, since the characters are keyed to the contemporary pronunciations of English words, which is precisely what the investigator is attempting to determine.

Ms. Haas also raised the question of the native language of the field workers and the possible influence of this upon their transcriptions. This, too, has its counterpart in our use of foreign-language grammars of English (i.e., grammars of English written for Frenchmen, Germans, Italians, etc.) as a source of evidence for contemporary pronunciation. Invariably, of course, the English pronunciations are keyed to words in the native language, be it French, German, or whatever, and this means that one must know the pronunciation of the foreign language at the time in order to arrive at a sound conclusion.

It would be possible to draw any number of additional parallels. They seemed to crop up on the average of one or two for every speaker. I think, however, that the point has been made: despite differences in the actual content of our various disciplines, we have a common set of problems and issues which override boundaries of both language and time. It has been helpful for all of us to bring these issues out of an internal awareness, which many of us may well have had, into an overt recognition. It has been equally beneficial to recall that the roles of linguist and philologist were once combined in one and the same person, and that even today the distance separating the two disciplines is by no means as great as we may have supposed.

I believe there is something to be learned as well from the successive combinations of linguistics with a number of other disciplines or fields of study. Here I am reminded of a most engaging essay by the late William R. Parker, who was for many years Executive Secretary of the Modern Language Association. In answer to the question posed by the title "Where Do English Departments Come From?," he commented that although English literary scholarship went back some three or four centuries, English departments as instructional units are very recent, and indeed, those in England are even more recent than those in the United States. This is equally true of linguistics, of course.

He then went on, somewhat playfully, to describe the English department as the product of a broken home. Its mother, the eldest daughter of Rhetoric, was Oratory. Its father was Philology or what we now call Linguistics. He suggests that the father had a happy affair with Anthropology, but that the mother entered into a disgraceful liaison with Elocution. Be that as it may, the thrust of the entire passage is that of successful and at times disastrous interdisciplinary combinations, and these are still going on.

The first attempt at getting psychologists and linguists together took place at Cornell University in the early 1950s. This first summer-long session began under the handicap of imperfect communication. Psychologists and linguists were simply not using the same language, the same terminology, and it took the entire summer to establish a bridge between them. Almost exactly ten years later history repeated itself, this time with the linguists and sociologists. Again, there were difficulties at the outset. At one point a frustrated linguist characterized sociologists as anthropologists who didn't know any languages. But ultimately a considerable degree of mutual understanding was achieved.

Just as linguistics has entered, successfully for the most part, into these interdisciplinary alliances, so it would seem high time that we begin to reunite the fields of philology and linguistics. At the conclusion of this conference I am certain that this, an admirable end in itself, can be done with much less difficulty than has been the case with some of the other disciplines with which linguistics has become allied.

NOTES ON CONTRIBUTORS

NOTE: These sketches try to highlight some of the activities and awards most representative of each participant's career. We could not record all achievements because of limitations of space.

AUSTERLITZ, Robert P. - Professor of Linguistics and Uralic Studies, Columbia University.

Born in Bucharest, Rumania in 1923, Professor Austerlitz came to the U.S. in 1938 and received his Ph.D. from Columbia University in 1955. After study in Finland and Japan, he joined the faculty of Columbia University in 1958. Seven years later he was appointed Chairman of the Linguistics Department there (a position he held for three years). Austerlitz has been a Visiting Professor at the Universities of Washington (Seattle, Linguistic Institute, summers, 1962, 1963), Yale (1964-5), California (Berkeley, 1969), and Ohio State (Linguistic Institute, summer 1970). He was a consultant to the Smithsonian Institution in 1967 on the map of language families in Eurasia, and was a Senior Fellow of the National Endowment for the Humanities in 1971-72. Austerlitz holds memberships in the Linguistic Societies of both America and Japan.

Austerlitz's linguistic interests focus primarily on phonetics, typology, and the history of the field. Other interests include the language and folklore of Northern Eurasia. He has written *Ob-Ugric Metrics* (1958) and is co-editor of *Readings in Linguistics II* (1966). He is currently editing—among other projects—Gilyak texts and vocabulary and hopes to publish a Gilyak grammar.

BAILEY, DAVID R. SHACKLETON - Professor of Greek and Latin, University of Michigan and Harvard.

David R. Shackleton Bailey was born in Lancaster, England, in 1917. He was educated at Lancaster Royal Grammar School and Gonville and Caius College, Cambridge, from which University he received a Litt.D. degree in 1957. He was a Fellow of Gonville and Caius College in 1944-55; Praelector in 1954-55; Deputy Bursar in 1964; and Senior Bursar in 1965-68. Shackleton Bailey has also been a Fellow and Director of Studies in Classics at Jesus College, Cambridge, and a Visiting Lecturer in Classics at Harvard (1963). From 1948-68 he was the University Lecturer in Tibetan at Cambridge. He joined the faculty of the University of Michigan as Professor of Latin in 1968, and holds membership in the British Academy since 1958. In January 1975 he moved to Harvard University.

Shackleton Bailey's publications include *The Satapañcasatka of Mātrceta* (1951), *Propertiana* (1956), *Towards a Text of Cicero ad Atticum* (1960),

Cicero (1971), and seven volumes of *Cicero's Letters to Atticus* (1960-70). In 1973-74 he was Visiting Andrew V. V. Raymond Professor of Classics at SUNY, Buffalo, where he taught Latin and Sanskrit while also working on an edition of Cicero's *Letters ad Familiares* and a translation of Cicero's correspondence for the Penguin series.

BARR, JAMES - Professor of Semitic Languages and Literatures, The University of Manchester, England.

A native of Scotland, Barr was educated at the University of Edinburgh where he studied first Classics and later Theology, particularly the Old Testament. He has taught in Canada (Montreal 1953-55), at the University of Edinburgh (1955-61), and at Princeton Theological Seminary (1961-65). Barr has lived and studied extensively in the Near East, especially in Israel, where he was a Visiting Professor at the Hebrew University (1972-73). In 1975 he was a Visiting Professor at the University of Chicago.

His main interest has been the semantic analysis of religious terminology in Biblical language. His two main works on this theme are *The Semantics of Biblical Language* (1961) and *Comparative Philology and The Text of the Old Testament* (1968). Other interests about which he has recently written include the reading techniques of scripts having no vowels; the language of religion; the analysis of etymological method; Philo of Byblos and his Greek history of the Phoenicians; the current ecological controversy and its relation to ancient religious views, especially those of the Old Testament.

Last year Barr published *The Bible in the Modern World* which explored the Bible in relation to modern faith. He is currently studying the expression of 'being' in Hebrew and the Biblical languages generally, and the history and description of the Hebrew language. He is engaged in detailed research in the technique of biblical translation in the ancient world, and in particular is Grinfield Lecturer on the Septuagint in the University of Oxford. His main research project, however, now lies in his work as Editor of the Oxford Hebrew Dictionary, a project sponsored jointly by the British Academy and the Oxford University Press.

GELB, IGNACE J. - Professor of Assyriology, Department of Linguistics and Oriental Institute, University of Chicago.

A native of Poland, Ignace J. Gelb received his doctorate from the University of Rome in 1929, the same year he settled in the United States. For the next four years he was a Travelling Fellow in the Oriental Institute of the University of Chicago. He has been a Professor in the Oriental Institute and the Linguistics Department of the University of Chicago since 1947; since 1965 he has been Frank P. Hixon Distinguished Service Professor. Gelb is a fellow of the American Academy of Arts and Sciences, the American Philosophical Society, and the Accademia Nazionale dei Lincei. He was a Visiting Professor at the University of Michigan in 1956 and 1967.

Professor Gelb holds honorary memberships in numerous international societies, such as the Société Asiatique of Paris, the Finnish Oriental Society, and the Institute of Asian Studies (India). He is also a member of several professional societies, and was national President of the American Oriental Society in 1959 and of the American Name Society in 1964. On the occasion of his 65th birthday, Gelb was offered a Festschrift entitled *Approaches to the Ancient Near East* at celebrations in Chicago and Los Angeles.

Gelb has published twenty-one monographs and over 200 articles in several research fields. His interest in Hittite hieroglyphs has resulted in four volumes, *Hittite Hieroglyphs* I, II, III and *Hittite Hieroglyphic Monuments.* His work in Old Akkadian has brought forth several volumes since 1952, including the recent *Sargonic Texts in the Ashmolean Museum* (1970). Professor Gelb has recently completed a monograph entitled *Between Freedom and Slavery.*

GOLDIN, JUDAH - Professor of Postbiblical Hebrew Literature, Department of Oriental Studies, University of Pennsylvania.

Judah Goldin was educated at the City College, Seminary College, and Columbia University in New York. He has received honorary degrees from the Jewish Theological Seminary and Yale University as well. He was Associate Professor of Religion at the University of Iowa from 1942 to 1952, spending two of those years (1943-45) as a Visiting Associate Professor of Jewish Literature and History at Duke University. Goldin has been Dean and Associate Professor of Aggadah at the Seminary College of the Jewish Theological Seminary of America (1952-58), Adjunct Professor of Religion at Columbia University (1955-58), and Professor of Classical Judaica at Yale (1958-73). He left Yale in 1973 to become Professor of Postbiblical Hebrew Literature in the Department of Oriental Studies at the University of Pennsylvania. He has held a Guggenheim Fellowship (1958), a Fulbright Research Fellowship (1964-65), and two grants from the American Philosophical Society (1957, 1971). He is a member of Phi Beta Kappa and a Fellow of the American Academy of Jewish Research.

Goldin has written a number of monographs and studies. His four books are: *The Fathers According to Rabbi Nathan* (1955), *The Living Talmud: The Wisdom of the Fathers* (1957), *The Jewish Expression* (ed. 1970), and *The Song at the Sea* (1971).

HAAS, MARY R. - Professor of Linguistics, University of California at Berkeley.

Mary R. Haas received her undergraduate training at Earlham College and her Ph.D. from Yale University in 1935, with an interim period of study at the University of Chicago (1930-31). She joined the Army Specialized Training Program at the University of California, Berkeley, in 1942, the Department of Oriental Languages in 1946, and participated in the founding of the Department of Linguistics in 1953 and has been associated with the latter ever since. She has been Department Chairman (1956-57; 1958-64), a Faculty Research Lecturer (1964-65), and Program Coordinator of the Survey of California Indian Languages (1964-   ). Haas has been a Visiting Professor at the University of Washington (Walker-Ames Professor, winter 1961), the University of Alberta (Summer Institute of Linguistics, 1967), the Ohio State University (Linguistic Society of America Professor, Linguistic Institute, summer, 1970), and at Barnard College and Columbia University (Virginia Gildersleeve Professor, spring 1971). She has been a Fellow of the American Council of Learned Societies (1941-43; 1044-46), the Center for Advanced Study of Behavioral Sciences at Stanford (1967-68), the Guggenheim Foundation (1964-65), and the National Endowment for the Humanities (Senior Fellow, 1967-68). She is a member of the Linguistic Society of America (President, 1963), the American Association for the Advancement of Science, and the American Oriental Society.

She has written a number of volumes on the Thai language, such as *Spoken Thai* (two volumes, with Heng Subhanka, 1946-48), *Thai Reader* (1954), *Thai Vocabulary* (1955) and *Thai English Student's Dictionary* (1964). Her books on Tunica include *Tunica Dictionary* (1953) and *Tunica Texts* (1949). Her latest book is *The Prehistory of Languages* (1969).

MARCKWARDT, ALBERT H.† - Professor of English, University of Michigan and Princeton.

Albert Marckwardt was educated at the University of Michigan, which awarded him a doctorate in 1933. He was associated with this University for much of his professional life, both as a Professor of English (1934-63) and as Director of the English Language Institute (1962-63). In 1963 he left Michigan to become a Professor of English and Linguistics at Princeton University; six years later Princeton appointed him Paton Foundation Professor Emeritus of Ancient and Modern Literature. In 1972 he returned to Ann Arbor to live.

In 1943-45 Marckwardt was Visiting Professor Extraordinary at the National Autonomous University of Mexico, and Director of the English Language Institute in Mexico. He held a Fulbright Lectureship at the Universities of Vienna and Graz (1953-54), and served on the U.S. Educational Commission in Japan (1968). As a State Department Consultant on Teaching English he held short appointments in Colombia (1943, 1968, 1969), Panama (1946), Italy (1954), Eastern Europe (1966), Peru (1970), and India (1971). He has held offices in the American Council of Learned Societies, the American Dialect Society, the Linguistic Society of America (President, 1967). A member of Phi Beta Kappa, Marckwardt received the Distinguished Faculty Service Award from the University of Michigan in 1962. Ten years later the National Council of Teachers of English awarded him a Distinguished Service Award, and in 1974 the State Department issued a Tribute of Appreciation to him.

Among his many publications are the *Scribner Handbook of English* (rev. 1967), *Linguistics and the Teaching of English* (1966), and *Old English: Language and Literature* (1972).

Professor Marckwardt died in London on August 20, 1975.

MERKELBACH, REINHOLD - Professor of Classics, University of Köln, Germany.

Professor Merkelbach was born at Höhr-Grenzhausen, Germany, in 1918. After receiving his doctorate from Hamburg in 1947, he taught at the University of Köln (1950-57), then transferred to Erlangen as a full professor (1957), returning to Köln four years later. Author and editor, Merkelbach has written *Untersuchungen zur Odyssee* (1951; second edition 1968), *Die Quellen des griechischen Alexanderromans* (1954), *Roman und Mysterium im Altertum* (1961). *Isisfeste* (1962), and recently *Emendationen und Erklärungen antiker Autoren* (1974), as well as many others. With M. L. West he edited the *Fragmenta Hesiodea* (1968). He is an Editor of *Zeitschrift für Papyrologie und Epigraphik* (18 volumes), *Papyrologische Texte und Abhandlungen* (15 volumes) and the massive *Beiträge zur klassischen Philologie* (63 volumes). His articles in English include those on mystery religions for the Encyclopedia Britannica and the British dictionary "Man, Myth and Magic," in addition to "Enchained Gods" for the *Yearbook of Comparative Criticism* (ed. Strelka).

PAPER, HERBERT H. - Professor of Linguistics and Near Eastern Languages, University of Michigan.

H. H. Paper, born in Baltimore, Maryland in 1925, received his B.A. (Classics) from the University of Colorado (1943), MA (Linguistics) from the University of Chicago (1948), and Ph.D. (Oriental Languages) from the same university (1951). A Fulbright Fellow to Iran in 1951-52, he served as epigrapher to the Mission Archéologique Française en Iran at Susa. His graduate training in Indo-European and Semitic linguistics, plus a dissertation on *The Phonology and Morphology of Royal Achaemenid Elamite,* involved him extensively in the whole field of cuneiform studies. After a year of research in Modern Persian at Cornell University, he joined the faculty of the University of Michigan in 1953, where he has taught a variety of language and linguistics courses. He became the first chairman of the Department of Linguistics at Michigan when that department was organized in 1963; and in the summers of 1965 and 1967 was Director of the Linguistic Institutes at Michigan. He has been active in both the Linguistic Society of America and the American Oriental Society. In 1959-60 he was a postdoctoral fellow of the American Council of Learned Societies at Cambridge University; and in 1968-69 he spent a sabbatical year in Jerusalem continuing his research into the Judeo-Persian language.

Paper's publications have included articles and monographs on various problems in Old Persian, Elamite, Modern Persian, and general linguistics. He has also published a number of translations of Russian grammars of Iranian languages. In recent years he has produced books and articles on Judeo-Persian texts, especially translations into that language of various parts of the Hebrew Bible. In 1975-76 he holds a Senior Research Fellowship from the National Endowment for the Humanities and is also a Guest Professor at the Hebrew University in Jerusalem.

PECKHAM, MORSE - Professor of English, University of South Carolina.

Born in Yonkers, New York in 1914, Morse Peckham was educated at the University of Rochester and at Princeton, where he received his doctorate in English in 1947. After teaching at The Citadel (1938-41) and at Rutgers University (1947-49), Peckham went to the University of Pennsylvania. There he was Director of the Institute for Humanistic Studies for Executives (1953-54), and Director of the University Press (1953-55). He remained at Pennsylvania until 1967, when he became Distinguished Professor of English at the University of South Carolina. He is a member of the Society of Architectural Historians as well as the Modern Language Association.

Peckham's publications range from criticism to scholarly editions. He is the Editor of *Charles Darwin's 'The Origin of Species': A Variorum Text* (1959) and of Algernon Charles Swinburne's *Poems, Ballads, and 'Atalanta in Calydon'* (1970). He has written *Beyond the Tragic Vision* (1962), *Man's Rage for Chaos* (1965), *Romanticism* (1965), *Art and Pornography* (1969), and *Victorian Revolutionaries* (1970).

RABIN, CHAIM - Professor of Hebrew Language, Hebrew University of Jerusalem.

Chaim Rabin was born in Germany in 1915 of Russian parents. He was educated in Germany and at the Universities of Jerusalem, London and Oxford. In 1939 he received a Ph.D. from the University of London in Arabic, and three years later a D. Phil. from Oxford. From 1941 to 1956 Rabin was Cowley Lecturer in Postbiblical Hebrew at the University of Oxford, and since 1956 has been a Professor of Hebrew Language at the Hebrew University of Jerusalem. He is a member of the Hebrew Language Academy.

Rabin is active in many projects for improving the teaching of modern Hebrew, such as the Ktav-Kol course on cassettes, and films for teaching Hebrew syntax through short plays for the Israel Educational Television. He is Chairman of the Council on the Teaching of Hebrew. Special interests include the influence of society on language development, religious language, and Indic loanwords in ancient Hebrew.

Rabin has written numerous articles in the fields of Semitic comparative grammar, Hebrew language history, etymology, semantics, syntax, and second language teaching. His books include *Ancient West-Arabian* (1951), *Qumran Studies* (1958), *The Zadokite Fragments* (1957), and *A Short History of the Hebrew Language* (1974). He is currently writing books on Ben-Yehuda, the history of the Hebrew language, and *The Hebrew Language Today,* an etymological dictionary of Biblical Hebrew. In 1973-74 he was on sabbatical leave at Oxford, with the new Oxford Centre for Postgraduate Hebrew Studies.